HOMEBREWED
BEERS &
STOUTS

FULL INSTRUCTIONS FOR ALL TYPES OF CLASSIC BEERS, STOUTS, AND LAGERS

C. J. J. Berr

FOX CHAPEL
PUBLISHING

First published in the United Kingdom by Special Interest Model Books, 1963.
First published in North America in 2011, updated and revised, by Fox Chapel Publishing, 1970 Broad Street, East Petersburg, PA 17520.

ISBN 978-1-56523-601-1

Library of Congress Cataloging-in-Publication Data

Berry, Cyril J. J.

Homebrewed beers & stouts / C.J.J. Berry.

  p. cm.

Originally published: [United Kingdom] : Special Interest Model Books, 1963.

Includes index.

ISBN 978-1-56523-601-1 (pbk.)

1. Brewing. 2. Cookbooks. I. Title. II. Title: Homebrewed beers and stouts.

TP570.B475 2011

663'.3--dc22

2011009668

To learn more about the other great books from Fox Chapel Publishing, or to find a retailer near you, call toll-free 800-457-9112 or visit us at *www.FoxChapelPublishing.com*.

Note to Authors: We are always looking for talented authors to write new books. Please send a brief letter describing your idea to Acquisition Editor, 1970 Broad Street, East Petersburg, PA 17520.

Printed in China
First printing: November, 2011

TABLE OF CONTENTS

Table of Contents (CONTINUED)

CHAPTER 1

ABOUT THIS BOOK

Today, home brewing is very much an accepted part of the social scene. Kits for brewing excellent bitters, pale ales, stouts, lagers, and specialist foreign beers are readily available from specialist shops, from chain stores, and online, and many people, perhaps spurred into the hobby initially by the ever-increasing cost of pub beers, have found that they can indeed, with the greatest of ease, brew at home really satisfying beers for at a relatively low cost. Why not join them?

Modern home brewing really took off in the 1960s. There was an upsurge in interest in home brewing and eventually beer kits started appearing on shop shelves to meet the demand. But there is much more to the hobby than just making up a kit. Home brewers need to know the theory behind the techniques they use, and how to devise their own formulations for any type of beer.

This book, first published in 1963, was the very first to cover in detail the home brewing of beers and stouts, and has become accepted as the ideal introduction to the subject. It has been welcomed by the thousands who wanted to brew their own wholesome beer, but were at a loss as to how to set about it, and well over half a million copies of the earlier editions have been sold.

Homebrewed Beers & Stouts has been continually updated since its first publication, of course, and this revised edition seeks to make the recipes and instructions more accessible to the American brewer. Originally published in the United Kingdom, most of the measurements throughout this book first appeared in British or metric form, and included the use of the British gallon (which is 5 quarts instead of 4) and British pint (which is 20 fl. oz. to the United States' 16 fl. oz. pint). While the metric and imperial measurements have not been removed from the text, all have been calculated and specified using the United States' system of measurement. Similar alterations have been made to specific words throughout the text, changing their spelling to reflect the American rather than the British style.

Regardless of the spelling of words, using this book, you will find that it is perfectly possible to brew a beer every bit as high in quality as that which can be obtained at your local bar, and the more you study the subject, the more you will realize why. You are using exactly the same ingredients as the commercial brewer, and similar methods, albeit on a smaller scale. There is no reason why you should not succeed. After all, at one time every public house, inn, and many a home brewed its own beer, and commercial brewing on a large scale is simply the product of modern times. Today, there remains a strong trend toward the old system of small breweries and home brewing.

Home brewing is a fascinating and rewarding pastime, undertaken intelligently, and this is the book to set you on the right track. Good brewing!

CHAPTER 2

BREWING VOCABULARY

Acetic acid:
The acid formed when beer is left exposed to the air and turns vinegary.

Acrospire:
Shoot that grows from grain of barley during malting.

Adjuncts:
Grains such as corn, rice, or wheat used to supplement the malt.

Ale:
Formerly unhopped beer. Currently refers to a top-fermented beer.

Attenuation:
The drop in a wort's specific gravity as sugar is used up during fermentation.

Barley:
Grain most commonly used for brewing, after malting.

Barley wine:
A very strong beer.

Barm:
Mixture of wort and yeast.

Barrel:
In the trade, a cask for holding 180 quarts (163.5 liters). The home brewer's plastic barrel holds 25-30 quarts (22.5-27 liters).

Beer:
Hopped ale.

Best bitter:
A high-quality pale ale.

Bottoms:
Deposits of yeasts and solids formed during fermentation.

Brewers' grains:
The insoluble residue of malt left in the mash tun after the wort has been run off.

Brewbin (Brew or fermentation bucket):
A 30-quart (27 liter) plastic bucket in which the wort is fermented.

Brewer's yeast:
A top-fermenting strain of *Saccaromyces cerevisiae*. This yeast ferments on the surface of the wort, forming floating islands of yeast that subsequently sink. Lager yeast (*S. uvarum*, previously *S. Carlsbergensis*) is bottom-fermenting.

Brown ale:
A medium-strength dark beer.

Burnt sugar:
Old name for caramel coloring. Prepared from glucose.

Burton water:
A description applied to water of similar hardness to that found at Burton-on-Trent, important in the brewing of pale ales.

Bush:
Ancient sign for an inn (hence: Good wine needs no bush). Probably of Roman origin; a "bush" of ivy and vine leaves was the symbol of the wine god, Bacchus.

Calcium sulfate:
One of the chemicals that gives water a permanent hardness. Popularly called gypsum or plaster of Paris.

Carbon dioxide:
Gas given off during fermentation that gives the head on beer, and the sparkle.

Caramel:
See *Burnt Sugar.*

Casks:
Butt, 540 quarts (491 liters); Puncheon, 360 quarts (327 liters); Hogshead, 270 quarts (245 liters); Barrel, 180 quarts (163.5 liters); Kilderkin, 90 quarts (82 liters); Firkin, 45 quarts (41 liters); Pin, 22.5 quarts (20 liters).

Condition:
The "life" a beer has owing to the carbon dioxide in it.

Cutting:
Stopping fermentation by adding finings.

Cytase:
Enzyme in barley grain that dissolves the cellulose protecting the granule and allows conversion to sugars.

Dextrins:
Non-fermentable sugars in wort released during mashing.

Diastase:
Enzyme in barley that converts starch to fermentable sugar.

Draught:
Beer served from the barrel.

Dry hopping:
Adding a few hops at the end of the boil to restore lost aroma.

Enzymes:
Catalysts in the barley grain that affect malting during the mashing process. (See also *Cytase, Diastase, Invertase, Maltase,* and *Zymase.*)

Fermentation:
Yeast working upon a sugar solution (the wort) to produce alcohol and carbon dioxide.

Fermentation lock:
A small water trap to allow the carbon dioxide from the fermentation to escape and to protect the brew from bacterial contamination.

Finings:
Used for removing suspended solids from cloudy beer; usually gelatin, isinglass, or Irish moss.

Flakes:
Corn, rice, or barley can be used as an adjunct to malt during mashing to modify the texture, head, and flavor of beer. They have already been precooked.

Fobbing:
Over-lively beer foaming up out of the bottle. Usually the beer has been kept in too warm a place, has been over primed, or the bottle has been overfilled.

Gallon:

8 imperial pints (about 4 liters), 160 fl. oz., or 277.25 cu. in. (American gallon, 8 U.S. pints, 128 fl. oz.). One imperial or English Gallon is equal to 1.25 U.S. gallons.

Gallon Comparison:					
English	1	2	3	4	5
American	1.25	2.5	3.5	4.75	6

Gill:

Usually ¼ imperial pint (142 ml.) of ale, but in some areas, a half pint.

Glucose:

Once sold as chips in light brown lumps, this is now more readily available as powder or syrup. Completely fermentable. Suited to dry beers and lagers.

Goods:

See *Grist*.

Gravity:

The density or weight of a liquid. (See *Original gravity* and *Specific gravity*).

Green malt:

Germinated barley before it is kilned.

Grist:

The blended grain used with barley after it has been malted and crushed. Also called goods.

Grit:

Any grain, other than barley, used in brewing. Raw and not prepared, like flakes.

Gypsum:

Calcium sulfate or plaster of Paris. An important constituent of water (or liquor) if beer is to clear well.

Hardness:

Quality in water desirable when brewing bitters or lights. See *Calcium sulfate*.

Head:

The froth on beer. Good head retention is important and is found in a well-conditioned beer with a good malt content, adequately hopped, because these factors contribute to its having sufficient surface tension.

Heading liquid:

Used for adding an artificial head.

Hop:
The flower of the hop plant (*Humulus lupulus*) used in beer for its preservative and flavoring qualities.

Hop oil:
A concentrate that can be used instead of dry hopping. It needs to be handled with care, for one drop is enough for up to 50 gallons (227 liters). Hop oil gives the beer an added zest.

Hydrometer:
Instrument for measuring the sugar content of a wort and strength of finished beer.

Hydrometer jar or Trial jar:
Jar in which hydrometer is floated for a reading to be taken.

Initial heat or Strike heat:
The temperature of the goods when the malt and hot water have just been mixed.

Invert sugar:
Sugar that has been inverted by hydrolysis in the presence of acid. Often used in final stages of brewing, or for priming, because it ferments well.

Invertase:
An enzyme that breaks down sucrose into glucose and fructose, thus inverting it and making it fermentable.

Irish moss or Copper finings:
A mixture of two marine algae, *Chondrus crispus* and *Gigartina mamillosa*, used as a clarifying agent. It functions as a coagulant for complex and unstable proteins.

Kiln:
Used in malting for drying and coloring malt after its germination.

Krausening:
Adding some vigorously fermenting wort to another wort that has almost fermented out; a way of priming beer.

Lactose:
Unfermentable sugar once used in sweet stouts.

Lees:
See *Bottoms.*

Length:
The volume to which the wort is diluted ready for fermenting.

Liquor:

In brewing, water.

Liter:

About 2 U.S. pints (1.75 imperial pints).

London water:

Soft water, as found in London, and suitable for brown ales and stouts.

Lupulin:

Yellow powder in the hop flower containing the oils and resins that give the hop its bitterness.

Malt:

Barley that has been treated as to convert its starch into fermentable sugar.

Malt extract:

Malt wort concentrated into a syrup of honey-like consistency or dry powder.

Maltose:

The fermentable sugar obtained by malting.

Mash:

Mixture of malt and hot water, or the combination of ingredients from which the beer will be made.

Mash tub (or tun):

Container for mash. A boiler or insulated container.

Milk stout:

Former name for a stout in which lactose (milk sugar) has been utilized for sweetening.

Nutrient:

Nitrogenous matter added to wort to boost the action of the yeast; yeast food.

Original gravity (OG):

The density of a liquid or wort before fermentation.

Pint:

Imperial pint: 20 fl. oz., reputed pint: a 12 oz. bottle, U.S. pint: 16 fl. oz.

Pitch:

To add yeast to the wort to cause fermentation.

Polishing:

Pressure filtration of beer to give it brilliance. Usually commercial practice only.

Priming:
  Adding a small quantity of sugar to a barrel or bottle of beer to cause a slight further fermentation and give it a head and sparkle.

Quart:
  A quarter-gallon (U.S.), about 1 liter.

Rack:
  To siphon beer off the lees into a fresh container; filling a cask.

Rouse:
  To stir or mix thoroughly, from bottom to top.

Sparging:
  Spraying the floating grains with hot water at the end of mashing, while the wort is drawn off from below.

Specific gravity (SG):
  The density or weight of a liquid compared specifically to that of water.

Strike heat:
  See *Initial heat.*

Torrified:
  Grains used as adjuncts, exploded like popcorn.

Trub:
  Sediment deposited after cooling wort.

Tun:
  Name given to many vessels in a brewery (mash tun). Once a measure (wine): 1,260 quarts (1,146 liters).

Ullage:
  The air space above the beer in a barrel.

Wort:
  The liquid extract ready to be fermented.

Yeast:
  The fermenting agent, in brewing usually a strain of *Saccharomyces cerevisiae.*

Zymase:
  The enzyme responsible for fermentation.

CHAPTER 3

THE STORY OF ALE AND BEER

What is ale or beer, and is there any difference?

It is perhaps only in this century that the two words "ale" and "beer" have come to mean almost the same thing. A more logical division of malt beverages today would be into "beers" and "stouts," hence the title of this book.

Today, "ale" and "beer" are virtually synonymous. Both denote a hopped alcoholic drink made from malted barley, but this was not always so. Originally, ale was malt liquor without hops, and the term beer was not in general use in the modern sense until hops were introduced in the fifteenth century. Beer, or *beor*, is mentioned in Anglo-Saxon writings, but it is not clear whether this was malt beer or a weak form of mead. And from the year 950 onward, the word *beor* seems to drop from the language, only to reappear as *bere* or *biere* in the fifteenth century.

Ale

Ale is used differently in various areas and can denote almost any malt liquor except stout and porter.

Ale was often brewed specifically for certain important occasions or festivals of old England. Thus, in rural life, there was Lamb-ale, for lambing time; Cuckoo-ale, for the day the first cuckoo was heard; Leet-ale, drunk in connection with the sitting of the old-time Courts, Baron and Leet; Harvest-ale for the gathering of the crops; October-ale; and Winter-ale. All in all, our forebears seem to have catered for most of the seasons. For university occasions there was Audit Ale, originally brewed at Trinity College, Cambridge, for audit day and subsequently, by other Oxford and Cambridge Colleges, Brasenose Ale and College Ale.

At one time, much brewing was in the hands of the Catholic Church, which sold ale to raise money for special purposes. The word ale, therefore, also came to be used to denote not only the actual drink, but also a special function or an occasion for fund-raising purposes—hence Church-ale for a parish event, Clerks-ale for Easter, Whitsun Ale, and Bride-ale. The proceeds from the sale of Bride-ale went to the bride. Similarly, there was Bid-ale, drunk at a party to which each guest brought a gift, and the reverse, Give Ale, a "free issue" bought as the result of a windfall or legacy.

Ancient Origins

Ale and beer, it is true to say, have been brewed in one form or another for thousands of years, not only from malted barley, but from corn and millet (in Africa) and rice (in Asia). Other grain has been and still is used either in place of barley or in addition to it.

Brewing is a craft that has its origins right back in the mists of antiquity. As long ago as 4000 B.C., beer was brewed in ancient Mesopotamia, where bread was mashed, malted, and fermented, and the resultant brew flavored with spices, dates, or honey.

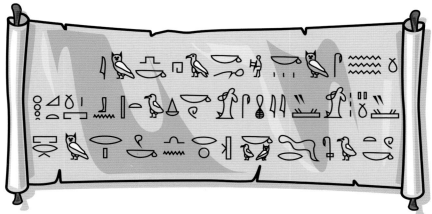

Reproduction of a dire warning contained in a 3,000-year-old Egyptian book of etiquette. It reads: Don't boast about your drinking prowess. Two jugs of beer and even you cannot understand what you're saying. When you fall over, nobody bothers to help you up. And your drinking companions, still upright, say, "Away with this sot."

According to legend, a thousand years or so later, Isis, the mother of the gods, introduced ale to Egypt, where at least six types of beer are thought to have been in daily use. The drink was known as *Boozah* or *Hequp* and became the popular national beverage. It was probably from ancient Egypt that barley was first brought to Britain, so perhaps the word "booze" came with it. It was probably a "bitter," because it is believed to have been flavored with rue. It is a whimsical thought that, in 3000 B.C., some now-forgotten Egyptian scribe set out to tackle exactly the same task as I do today.

The Greek word for ale was *zythos,* and the Romans called it *cerevisia.* In Spain, the drink is called *cerveza,* and in parts of France, even today, the old name for beer (*cervoise*) is still used instead of the modern *bière,* which derives from the German. *Cerevisia* stood originally for a weak mead, or honey beer, and the word is seen again in the Latin name for brewer's yeast—*saccharomyces cerevisiae.* Ceres was the goddess of wheat and the harvest and we still see the same root word in "cereal." The Romans had beer as well as wine as an everyday drink, and rated it highly. Lucullus, the classic epicure, served it in golden goblets at his banquets, and Julius Caesar gave it to his successful commanders.

Fermented drinks of one sort or another were being brewed in Britain before recorded history began, but they were probably meads made from the honey of wild bees. It is not clear whether any malt liquors were made before the Roman invasion, but certainly during the 400 years of the Roman occupation, ale was consumed in quantity in Britain, for many of the members of the Roman Legion were recruited from elsewhere in Europe, where beer was one of the essentials of life. The Romans may thus have introduced the British to ale and the hop. Certainly the Britons, the Picts, and the Scots all knew how to brew, and ale was served at their feasts and important celebrations.

When the Romans left and the Saxons and Vikings descended upon Britain, brewing was one craft that persisted, for the North men were lovers of ale, quaffing it from drinking horns before battle and in their redoubtable feastings.

Ale houses became numerous, so much so that Edgar the Peaceable, King of Wessex, had many of them closed, ordaining that there should not be more than one per village. At this period, too, drinking mugs were marked with pegs to define the size of a swig and facilitate drinking contests. Hence the origins of the phrase, *taking someone down a peg.*

The Normans were also no strangers to malt liquor, and in the settled centuries after the conquest, brewing for the first time became feasible on a really large scale. Mostly it was the province of the monasteries and Church. The Domesday Book, for instance, records that the monks of St. Paul's Cathedral brewed 81,441 gallons (U.S.), or 308,289 liters, of ale from 175 quarters each of wheat and barley and 708 quarters of oats. One cannot be exact because of variations in measures, but that would probably be three times as strong as modern beers. Knowledge of brewing was even more widespread than it is today, and every housewife could turn her hand to it.

The first tax on ale (Henry II's impost on movables) was levied in 1188, and from then on, there were various enactments to control both quality and price, such as Henry III's Assize of Bread and Ale (1267), which tied the price of these commodities to those of grain and malt, and which lasted for three centuries. Heavy penalties were imposed upon bakers or brewers whose products did not come up to the mark in quantity or quality. As a result, in the fourteenth century we see the introduction of that well-known official, the ale-conner, or ale-taster.

At this time there was, of course, no mechanical way of assessing a brew's worth, so the ale-taster had authority to taste any brewer's ale and order its price to be lowered if it was not satisfactory. The ale-conner (or *al-konnere*) wore leather breeches, and the practical test he employed was to pour some beer on a barrel end and sit on it for a specified period. If, when he rose, his breeches stuck momentarily to the barrel, the sweet beer was not up to standard (although some schools of thought indicate that this meant the beer *was* up to standard).

Incidentally, right up until England's local government reorganization in 1973, my own borough of Andover had an official ale-taster who was solemnly appointed at mayor-making each year (but he no longer took the oath of office and certainly did not wear leather breeches).

The Middle Ages were a great period of expansion and improvement in brewing. Ale was the national beverage. Honey was the common sweetener, because sugar did not become popularly available until the middle of the eighteenth century. At first, each ale house brewed its own beverage, but gradually, breweries sprang up, each supplying several houses. In time, these grew in size and importance.

Brewing had become an accepted craft, and was given standing in England by royal decree in 1406, when the Worshipful Company of Brewers (which still exists) was recognized as "the Mistery of Free Brewers." In 1437, the company was granted a charter by Henry VI to exercise control over "the brewing of any kind of malt liquor in the City and its suburbs for ever."

Beer

It was in the fourteenth century, too, that hops were introduced and the word beer reappeared. Previously, Britain had drunk the fermented malt drink called ale, but soldiers returning from the Hundred Years War (1338-1453) missed and demanded the drink to which they had become accustomed in northern France and Flanders: *bere* or *bière.* This was an ale flavored with hops, which then grew only on the Continent and not in Britain (where they were not planted before 1525). The Romans may have used them, but after their departure, ale was flavored in many ways with other herbs—nettles, rosemary, alecost (costmary), gruit (a mixture of herbs), or even ground ivy.

Like all innovations, the hop was bitterly opposed by the traditionalists, and there was fierce competition between ale-brewers and beer-brewers. The former brought all possible pressures to bear against the use of the "wicked, pernicious weed." They managed to have legislation passed that only water, malt, and yeast could be used in the production of ale, and it was not until 1493 that beer brewers were given craft recognition as a guild.

There were no indigenous hops in England, and the Kentish hop fields were cultivated from 1524 to 1525 by immigrants from the Lowlands, leading to the suggestion in Sir Richard Baker's *Chronicles of the Kings of England* concerning 1524:

"Tyrkeys, Carps, Hops, Piccarel, and Beer,

Came to England in one year."

Once the hop was introduced (originally as a preservative), it grew more and more popular until it eventually became an essential part of the accepted flavor of beer. This process, however, took two or three centuries, and the old flavors persisted side by side with it. It is, as I have said, perhaps only in this century that ale and beer have finally come to mean the same.

Gin Lane, William Hogarth, c. 1751

The first licensing laws seem to have been introduced by Henry VII in 1495, and in 1552 Edward VI passed measures to control "taverns and tippling houses."

The Tudors, including Henry VIII, and the "first" Elizabethans, including Good Queen Bess, were all great beer drinkers (in those days one had beer for breakfast), and beer has, despite all of its rivals, really remained the national favorite ever since. The seventeenth century saw the introduction of fortified wines, such as sherry and port, and of brandy. Because these were favored by the "upper crust," beer tended to be drunk less often at formal or official functions, though it remained the everyday drink of the nation.

It was a Stuart, Charles I, who imposed the first really effective taxation on beer in 1643, a trend that was continued by Charles II and his successors until nearly half the national income was derived from this source.

This went hand in hand with the development of brewing, which accelerated greatly in the eighteenth century. The middle of the century saw many famous breweries founded—Barclay, Bass, Charringtons, Coombe, Courage, Guinness, Meux, Simonds, Watney, Whitbread, and Worthington, for instance—and brewing became a truly big business, with a really impressive export trade.

This, of course, attracted yet more taxation on beer, malt, and hops, which in turn drove the people to drink cheap spirits (in England gin, in Scotland whisky). This led to the dissolute period savagely lampooned by Hogarth in *Gin Lane* and *The Rake's Progress.*

In an effort to better conditions—and to improve the government's popularity—taxes on beer were abolished in 1830, though those on malt and hops were retained. Licensing laws were introduced in 1839 and have been constantly amended ever since. The use of sugar in brewing was legalized in 1847.

The tax on hops was dropped in 1862, and the impact of science on the growing brewing industry made it possible for then Prime Minister William Ewart Gladstone, in 1880, to abandon the tax on malt and introduce beer taxation based on specific gravity (SG) and the use of the hydrometer (or saccharometer).

At this time, beers were strong, with gravities such as: strong ales 1083-1116; Russian Stout 1116-1131; porter 1069-1083; pale ale 1055-1069.

It was Gladstone's 1880 Act, incidentally, that applied to the home brewer, "the private brewer not for sale," a status that was determined by the measurable value of one's premises. Because this measurable value eventually became out of date and was not amended, the act became meaningless, but it remained on the Statute Book, producing an incredibly complicated and unsatisfactory situation for would-be home brewers, right up until 1963, when then Chancellor of the Exchequer, Reginald Maudling, removed all restrictions on home brewing.

Modern Beers

This century, of course, has seen the disappearance of hundreds of small breweries and the emergence of mammoth brewery combines. This has meant the disappearance of many once-popular and highly individual brews and a gradual flattening out of variations in beers until only a few main types now survive. Draught beer once was king, and the most popular English beer was mild, which could be drunk all evening without too much of a hangover. As with all draught beer in wooden barrels, however, mild's condition depended largely on the cellar work of the landlord. Today huge breweries bring science to their aid and, more and more, beer is artificially conditioned, and the trend is steadily moving toward keg beers. The Campaign for Real Ale (CAMRA), has in some measure reversed the trend by creating a demand for beer that has not been artificially carbonated. Modern keg beers, while they may not be so strong (because of the effects of taxation) are at least of consistent quality. Home brewers, however, can have both quality and strength. Beer drinking in the UK has grown to the extent that, as a nation, we now spend some ten billion pounds a year on beer.

Bottled beers, introduced just before World War I, have grown steadily in popularity, and in modern times, canned beer sales have rocketed in the same way.

But by far the biggest change in the popularity stakes has been seen in lager sales, lager now displacing bitter as Britain's most popular drink, no doubt due to some consistently clever advertising and sales promotions in recent years.

CHAPTER 4

TYPES OF BEER AND STOUT

Nowadays it is perfectly possible to brew at-home beers similar to most of the well-known name brands. If you wish to carry your brewing knowledge that far and try experimenting on those lines, it will pay you to read Dave Line's excellent book *Making British-Style Beers and Ales (*earlier editions were titled *Brewing Beers Like Those You Buy).* But any brewer certainly needs to be able at least to recognize the principal types popular today, because they are the ones that appeal to the modern palate.

Ordinary ale or beer may be anywhere between three percent and six percent alcohol by volume, so its average original gravity (OG) will have been about 1030.

Other beers may be stronger, and therefore more expensive, because more malt will be used in their production and they may need longer storage.

The following is a list of ales and beers you are likely to encounter in today's market:

Best Bitter: A general term for what is perhaps the highest expression of the brewer's craft, embracing Light Ale, Pale Ale, Indian Pale Ale, and others of similar type, varying according to strength and hopping. All are straw-colored, dry, have a good bite, and are popular as bottled beers. Only the lightest and finest barleys, giving a pale malt, are used, and the relatively large amount of hops used gives a pronounced hop flavor, giving this beer its description as bitter.

Light Ale: As its name implies, this is light in both color (straw) and texture. Smooth, dry, and well hopped, with a good bite. Should be brilliant and have good head retention. Original gravity is about 1030.

Pale Ale: Slightly more body than light ale, slightly more strength (OG anywhere between 1040 and 1045). Slightly more hops and slightly more color

(straw to light amber). India Pale Ale was originally specially brewed in the nineteenth century to be sent to British troops in India at the time of the British Raj. Burton Ale (no longer necessarily brewed in Burton-on-Trent) has an OG of 1045, while bottled pale ales have one of about 1033. Pale ale should be high in malt bouquet, and well hopped, with a dry fresh clean taste.

Mild Ale: Varies enormously according to locality, but is usually less strong than bitter, darker in color, less bitter (less hops), and slightly sweeter. Can be almost dark brown in color. OG is about 1030, and the alcohol content is three percent to three and a half percent. Once called Four-Ale, it is now slowly regaining its lost popularity.

Brown Ale: Can be similar to mild, but is usually slightly heavier and stronger (e.g. Newcastle Brown, Stock Ale, and Scotch Ale). Made from dark malts, kilned at high temperatures, and perhaps roasted. OG 1040.

Old Ale: Not quite so heavy or dark as most brown ales, but of high alcohol content and well matured. OG 1045.

Barley Wine: Very high in alcohol content (OG about 1080, that of a dry wine); color preferably deep garnet; full, fruity bouquet, and an almost vinous flavor. Long maturation is necessary.

Stout: A peculiarly British drink, not brewed in continental Europe. Dry type: As drunk in Ireland, it has about five percent alcohol, derived from an OG of about 1045. It is very dark, almost black, and is made from much-roasted (or torrified) barley, and the head is full and creamy. The bouquet is full and the taste sharply woody or bitter, as the result of high hopping and the use of roasted malts. Sweet-type stout is similar to ordinary stout, but sweetened with caramel or lactose. Milk Stout is not made partly from milk, and the name has now been abandoned. It was so called because lactose, the type of sugar found in milk, is used in its manufacture. The blackest, strongest, and most popular Extra Stout is made from the most heavily roasted malts and is extremely difficult to imitate.

Porter: First made in 1722 (it was then known as Entire) and became popular in the eighteenth and nineteenth centuries, and is still popular in Ireland. It is a mixture of ale, beer, and two-penny, a pale small beer. In appearance, it is halfway between ale and stout and, as far as can be discovered, derives its name from the fact that it was the favorite tipple of market porters in London. (Porterhouse steaks were sold at the porterhouse, the tavern where porter was sold.) It is made with soft water and the OG nowadays is about 1040.

Lager: Surprisingly enough, is quite difficult to make successfully from basic ingredients (as opposed to kits), for it is not just a light weak beer, as so many think, but the product of a rather different brewing system. British beers are produced by infusion and top fermentation, whereas lager, the popular drink in continental Europe and in America, is produced by decoction and bottom fermentation, with a slow secondary fermentation at a low temperature during the several months for which it is stored. In other words, it is a beer produced by a winemaking fermentation technique. The yeast employed is a special one, *Saccharomyces uvarum* (previously known as *S. Carlsbergensis)* now available to the home brewer, and the hops are likewise usually special ones—Hallertauer or Saaz. The hopping rate is only about half that of beer. Color should be straw (though there are some dark lagers to be found in Bavaria) and the lager should be lively with good head retention. OG is about 1060. The taste is light, smooth, and clean, with plenty of malt and not too much hops.

CHAPTER 5

BACKGROUND TO BREWING

Brewing is a process of producing an alcoholic drink through the fermentation by yeast of a flavored sugary solution. When yeast, a living organism, is put into a solution containing sugar and certain other essentials, it feeds upon the sugar to obtain the energy it needs for self-reproduction. A by-product of this reproductive process is the alcohol we seek.

As the yeast multiplies, it converts the sugar in the liquid half to alcohol and half to gas (carbon dioxide) by weight, the gas providing the sparkle and head so much admired in a good beer.

With beers, the final alcoholic strength may be anywhere between three percent and about six percent. By increasing the sugar content, we can increase the strength to eight percent and even ten percent so the beer is really a barley wine. It should be noted, however, that popular preference has always been for the weaker beers, because your beer drinker usually prefers quantity to strength.

In orthodox commercial brewing (as distinct from the making of simplified beers from kits, malt extract, or ingredients other than barley) the basic material for providing the sugar is grain, such as barley, which contains starch. Starch in its original state is not fermentable by the yeasts we wish to employ, so it has first to be converted to sugar, which is fermentable.

This is done by germinating the barley (malting), lightly milling it, and steeping it in hot water, or liquor (mashing). This sets up a chemical action that converts the starch in the malt to soluble carbohydrates, making sugar (maltose or dextrose) available for fermentation.

When studying the home production of beer, it is a great help to take a quick look at what happens in commercial brewing, for if we fully know the basic processes, we are that much less liable to go wrong with our home brew.

Commercial breweries take beer making to the level of mass production.

Commercial Brewing

Malting

After the barley has been cleaned and all dust and foreign bodies removed, it has to be malted, or germinated. The grain is steeped in water for two or three days and, as it absorbs moisture, swells and softens. Surplus water is drained off and the grain is then malted, or germinated, in large drums that allow easy control of warmth and ventilation. The barley germinates and a tiny shoot, the acrospire, starts to grow within from the base of the grain, and a gas, carbon dioxide, is given off.

Germination and growth may continue for about ten days, at temperatures ranging from 55.5°F-62.5°F (13°-17°C), with plenty of aeration, by which time the acrospire, still within the husk, will be about three-quarters the length of the grain. Growth of this green malt is then terminated. This is done by kilning, a drying process. Moderate heat is employed at first (122°-158° F, 50°-70° C), and then the temperature is raised to wither the shoot and, perhaps, lightly or heavily roast the malt. Final temperatures are lower for pale malts (176°F-185°F, 80°-85° C) than for dark malts (over 212°F, 100° C). It is at this stage, by delicate variations of temperature, timing, and method, that different flavors can be treated and a whole range of pale, crystal, brown, and black malts produced. The green malt may be kilned over wood chips, heated in an oven, or even roasted fully.

The kilning process is obviously a tricky one for the average home brewer, who dodges it by buying ready malted grain and thus starts with the next process that occurs in the brewery.

Cracking

The malt is then ground, or lightly crushed between rollers. At this stage, it is known as "grist" (hence *grist to the mill*).

Mashing

This, it must be emphasized, is the most important single operation in brewing, for it is here that the principal enzymatic change occurs in the malt. Enzymes are biological catalysts, or agencies within the grain that have power to change

other substances without themselves being changed, and there are several that
have to play a part. The enzyme cytase dissolves the protective cellulose coating
of the barley granules, giving access to the starch, which the enzyme diastase then
liquefies and converts to fermentable sugar (or maltose) and dextrins, which
dissolve in the water to form a sweet malt-flavored liquid known as sweet wort.

Enzyme activity is extremely sensitive to temperature changes, so by varying
conditions during mashing of the beer, the brewer is able to vary the wort and,
therefore, the resultant beer. The temperature in the mash tun must be between
145° and 155°F (62°-68°C).

The grist is mixed with hot water in the mash tun, and other grits, such as
flaked barley, oats, or corn may be added. The temperature of the mixture is
maintained at 144°F-154°F (62°-68°C) for at least two hours. During this time,
the principal starch-to-sugar conversion takes place.

Then the sweet wort is run off from the bottom of the mash tun and, at the
same time, the mash is sprayed (or sparged) from above with hot water, to wash
out trapped wort.

Boiling

The wort is then boiled with the hops at the rate of 1 lb.-5 lb. (450 g.-2.25 kg.)
hops per barrel of 180 quarts (164 liters). This process stabilizes the wort by
sterilizing it and preventing further enzyme activity. It also concentrates it to
the required strength and extracts the preservative and flavoring qualities of the
hops. Because some of these are volatile and would be driven off, it is usual to
"dry hop" or add some hops toward the end of this process. Boiling also assists
eventual clarification by precipitating some of the complex malt proteins. From
the boiler, the wort is pumped to the "hop back," another vessel with a false
bottom. The hops settle onto this and form a natural filter bed, through which
the hopped wort drains on its way to the coolers and fermenting vessels.

Fermenting

The wort is cooled down to about 60°F (15°C), run into large fermenting vessels,
and the yeast is "pitched." Top-fermenting yeast is used (except for lager) and
the fermentation lasts about a week. When it is completed, the beer is skimmed
to remove top yeast and racked into storage vessels.

Conditioning

The cloudy draught beer (cloudy because yeast is still in suspension in it) is then fined, or rendered brilliant, by the use of isinglass, the flocculent fragments of which settle gradually, carrying down the suspended solids and leaving the clear beer above. Other conditioning, such as the addition of dry (unboiled) hops to pale ales, is practiced to improve flavor and aroma and to meet public taste. Treatment of the beer at this stage varies widely. Mild ales usually leave the brewery only a few days after they have been racked and are often sweetened (or primed). Bottled beers and strong beers, however, may be stored for weeks or months, during which there may be a slow secondary fermentation. Many home brewers puzzle over how to obtain a clear bottled beer with a good head, but without yeast deposit. The brewery overcomes the problem by fining the beer, chilling it, and saturating it with carbon dioxide under pressure.

Having seen what the commercial brewers do, let us see how we can adapt their methods for use in our home.

Keep It Clean

Make sure all your equipment, fermenters, bottles, kegs, and siphon tubes are clean, and your workplace is kept free of drips and splashes. Nothing grows a mold or breeds infection more quickly than spilled beer. Damp beer bottles are particularly dangerous and should be carefully inspected both inside and out, and stoppers, when reused, should always be boiled or sterilized.

For simple cleaning of brewing apparatuses (as distinct from sterilizing) one can use a solution made up of 4.25 oz. (125 g.) of washing soda (sodium carbonate) or of 1 fl.oz. (30 ml.) of chlorine bleach in 5 quarts (4.5 liters) of water. Rinse well afterward.

For simple sterilizing (as distinct from cleaning), one can use sodium or potassium metabisulfite. Make up a stock solution by dissolving 3 oz. (90 g.) of the crystals in 1 quart (1 liter) of water (or 2 oz. in 1 pint, 55 g. in 500 ml.). This gives a ten percent solution, which can be kept for convenience in a discarded plastic bottle previously used for washing up liquid. When you want some solution for sterilizing your equipment, give a two-second squirt from your bottle into 1 pint (500 ml.) of water and it will be about right. Keep the squirt-bottle sealed when not in use.

Alternatively, dissolve six Campden tablets and ½ oz. (15 g.) citric acid in 1 pint (500 ml.) of water. Keep it in a sealed bottle and avoid inhaling, because it is very pungent. This solution soon loses its strength.

My own method is to combine both washing and sterilizing. I do this by using a proprietary powder, Chempro, liberally. It cleans glassware, plastic, and stainless steel magically in a few minutes and the washed equipment only requires a good rinse afterward. This takes all the donkey work out of the business. VWP's and VINA's cleaner/sterilizers are similar products.

For cleaning bottles, a regular job, I merely fill the sink with hot water and stir in two tablespoons of Chempro, a cleaner, sterilizer, and deodorizer sold commercially. Bottles are given a good soak—all stoppers are thrown in loose as well—and then well rinsed in plain water and drained in a rack before use.

Cleanliness is essential, and you can use many different products depending on your preference, including sodium metabisulfite for cleansing and products from VWP for sterilizing.

Sterilizing brewing and storage containers
is necessary for good beer.

CHAPTER 6

SOME IMPORTANT POINTS

Balanced Formulations

Some important principles to remember in arriving at the formulation of any beer:

1. The more malt, the more body, strength, and head retention.
2. The more body, the more hops needed.
3. The more hops, the greater the bitterness and hop aroma.
4. The more sugar (household), the greater the strength, but the thinner the beer if used instead of malt.
5. Never forget the importance of adequate boiling of the wort in producing quality beers.
6. The sooner bottled, the greater the risk.

Strength

Now may I sound a warning? Do not make your beer too strong.

At first sight, this may appear to be extraordinary advice. "Surely the whole point of brewing my own beer," you may well ask, "is that by doing so, I can have a better beer than I can buy?" "Better," for most people, is at first synonymous with "stronger."

But strength is even less the principal criterion of a good beer than it is of a good wine.

After all, extra strength is easy enough to achieve. One has merely to use more malt or sugar and ferment for a longer period, and it is quite feasible to produce a beer of, say, wine strength, up to ten percent to fourteen percent alcohol by volume.

But is it desirable? Breweries will tell you that their strongest beers are by no means the most popular, and the answer does not lie simply in the fact that they are more expensive. Until recent years, the most popular beer in Britain was for a long time the weakest—mild, although today it has been supplanted by lager, itself not unduly strong.

Why is this? Surely the answer lies in the beer drinker's approach to his drinking. The beer drinker, unlike the wine lover, expects to be able to drink a fair quantity, say 3 or 4 pints (1.5-2 liters), without ill effect. It should make him pleasantly relaxed, but not make him drunk or leave him with a splitting headache the following day.

Any beer drinker who has had an evening out drinking a high gravity (i.e., strong quality beer) will know what I mean. That is why your habitual beer drinker prefers the lower-gravity bitters and milds. He can drink them for a whole evening's celebration without risk.

Surely the same is true of homebrewed beer? It is neither wise nor hospitable to brew beer so strong that after two glasses your friend slips under the table or has a severe headache the next day. He will not thank you for it. Homebrewed beers are not a whit inferior to commercial ones, but they were once upon a time often made far too strong, with disastrous results upon host or guest, which earned them a quite undeserved bad reputation. Luckily, the increasing use of kits is correcting this, because they produce beers of the proper strengths.

Aim at making your brews of roughly the same strength as the principal commercial types you are emulating, and do not fall into the error of making them so very strong. If you must produce double-strength beer, or barley wine, then please treat it with respect. Warn your friends of its strength, and serve it in smaller glasses, not in pint glasses or tankards.

You have been warned.

Obtaining a Head

One of the principal difficulties that amateur brewers encounter with bottled beers is that of obtaining a good head, which does so much to make a home brew look attractive. It is easy, by bottling prematurely, to produce a beer with a foaming uncontrollable head, far more suitable for extinguishing fires than topping a tankard. It is also easy, by bottling too late and adding no priming sugar, to produce a beer that is as strong as the sugar used allows, but flat.

The secret is to ferment the beer almost to completion (i.e., to a specific gravity of between 1005 and 1010), and then, when bottling, to add just enough priming sugar to produce a sparkle and head. Usually this means half a heaping teaspoon of sugar per pint (500 ml.). If head retention is poor, it is probably due to using poor quality malt, using insufficient amounts of malt, or of not having allowed the beer to mature.

One can solve the problem by adding a heading liquid, which can be purchased from suppliers with full instructions. This, while it gives an artificial head, does not seem to impart life to the beer, and is therefore not so satisfactory.

CHAPTER 7

BREWING FROM KITS

There are four main approaches to brewing at home, and they are (in order of simplicity, but not of quality or economy):

1.   A kit (wet or dry)

2.   Malt extract

3.   Mashing (using grain malt and other grits)

4.   A combination of the second and third

There is no doubt that the great majority of those taking up home brewing first do so by buying a proprietary beer kit, and this is certainly a wise way to start, because it is the ultimate in simplification.

There is an abundance of homebrew kits available to enable one to produce a range of beers. Many of them are excellent and can be used to produce bitters, best bitters, stouts, brown ales, lagers, and more.

Quality tends to vary according to price, as one would expect, but there is no denying that the leading kits give one beers that are every bit as good as commercial brands, and often better and stronger. The great majority of kits are 4 lb. (2 kg.) cans, most of which call for the addition of 2 lb. (1 kg.) of sugar, and which make perfectly satisfactory beers and lagers for a reasonable price. The latest development is the introduction of 7 lb. (3.5 kg.) cans, to which no sugar has to be added. Some have the sugar included as syrup, but most are wholly malt, giving a fuller-bodied and better-flavored beer.

Most of the kits are very simple to use, because they consist principally of a 4 lb. (2 kg.) can of concentrated wort, which is already hopped, and which makes 40 pints (20 liters) of beer. At one swoop, therefore, the processes of mashing and hop boiling are eliminated, and the whole business of brewing is

reduced to little more than adding water (some hot, some cold) and yeast, and then fermenting, priming, and bottling.

One or two dry kits are obtainable that employ malt, or dried malt extract, with hops. These make good beers, but do involve longer boiling times.

The great advantage of the modern kit is that it streamlines your brewing and gives you a consistent assured result. In almost all kits, the instructions are simple and straightforward and obviously, whichever kit you buy, those are the ones to follow for the first few times. (Subsequently, as your experience grows, you may well be able to make minor adjustments to the formulation to suit your particular taste, e.g., by increasing or decreasing strength, by dry hopping, or by increasing or decreasing carbonation.)

Equipment

The beauty of starting with a kit beer is that you need the minimum of gear and can therefore try your hand at brewing with the least expense.

All you need is:

1. A 5-quart (4.5 liter) saucepan (or larger)

2. A brewbin able to hold 25-30 quarts (22.5-27 liters)

3. A siphon tube

4. A hydrometer

5. Forty 1-pint (500 ml.) returnable beer bottles (do not use no-deposit bottles)

You do not need a lot of special equipment for home brewing. A few basic essentials can get you started right away.

Other small items such as scales, a large kitchen spoon, a funnel, and a thermometer you probably already have in your kitchen. Some would argue that even a hydrometer is not truly necessary, but I think that, for the small sum it costs, it is invaluable to the beginner, for it tells him exactly when to bottle his beer, and thus enables him to avoid over-lively beer and burst bottles or containers.

Kit beers differ only from extract or mash beers in the preliminary stages, i.e., in the preparation of the wort.

With most kits, it is necessary to bring a few pints of water to boil, and the hopped wort extract is then dissolved in the water and boiled for a short time. Sometimes the addition of sugar is recommended so that a stronger beer is obtained, but beware of kits that advocate too little malt and a high proportion of sugar. The more malt and the less sugar, the better the kit, as a rule.

The hot wort is then poured into the brewbin and made up to the correct length (usually 20 or 25 quarts, 18 or 22.5 liters) with warm or cold water, and is then allowed to cool. From then on, the brewing process is the same as for ordinary extract or mashed malt beers. (Many brewers today use an alternate process in which they boil the full quantity of water, about 25 quarts (22.5 liters) or so, and then add the malt extract and boil again. Hops can also be added to the wort at this stage, and the wort boiled again.)

When the temperature has dropped to 75°F (24°C), the yeast is introduced and the brewbin covered and stood in a warm place (64.5°-71.5°F, 18°-22°C).

Fermentation usually takes about five days, during which time the specific gravity of the wort (see pg. 69) will attenuate from the initial 1035 or 1040 down to below 1010, and preferably to 1005.

The beer is then siphoned into bottles (or a plastic barrel) and priming sugar added at the rate of ½ a heaping teaspoon per pint (500 ml.) bottle or 2½ oz. (70 g.) per 25-quart (22.5 liter) barrel. Instructions for various kits may differ slightly (some add finings), but this is the general procedure.

The beer is usually ready for drinking after two weeks, but barrels take longer to clear because the yeast has further to fall. You can buy a float attachment for your barrel that draws the beer from near the surface, so you don't have to wait for the whole barrel to clear.

Making A Kit Beer

1. Warm the extract to make pouring easier by standing the can in hot water.

2. Pour the extract into the fermentation bucket.

3. Add hot water and dissolve the extract.

4. Top up the wort to the desired quantity with filtered cold water.

5. Stir thoroughly with a plastic paddle.

6. Check the specific gravity of your wort with your hydrometer. Most beers have starting gravities of 1035-1045 (35°-45°).

Chapter 8

Brewing Ingredients

Having tried a beer kit, you will probably soon wish to try your hand at formulating some of your own beer, thereby reducing expense still further. To do that you will need to know more about possible ingredients and equipment.

Principal ingredients, of course, are malt, hops, water, and yeast (and often added sugar and grains), so let us look at each in detail.

Malt

You can, if you wish, malt your own barley at home and produce, say, 5 or 6 lbs. (2.25-3 kg.) of malt, sufficient to make about 25-30 quarts (22.5-27 liters) of beer. Buy good round-grained barley free of impurities, but before you go to the bother of malting all of it, do a trial run to see if it will germinate. Take a few grains and soak them in water for twenty-four hours, then lay them between blotting paper in a warm place such as a propagator or a not too hot airing cupboard. They should sprout after a week or so.

If all goes well and the barley germinates, you can go ahead and malt the bulk, following the same procedure. Soak all the grain in some water in a plastic bucket at a temperature of 60°F (16°C) for forty-eight hours, changing the water four or five times. Then lay out the wet grain between damp newspapers, at a temperature of 60°-65°F (16°-18°C), and make sure it stays just damp and does not dry out. After a week or so, you should see the acrospire or growing shoot as a bulge halfway up the husk, which means that germination has been effected.

Put the grain on racks or trays in an oven with the door open and kiln or roast gently at 120°F (49°C) for twelve hours. Turn the grains from time to time to achieve an even kilning. Do not overdo the process or you will destroy enzymes in the malt, which will be needed during mashing when brewing.

As will be seen, this is a rather fussy business, and most home brewers prefer to buy their malt (ready malted barley) from a reliable homebrew supplier. It can be supplemented or reinforced by the use of malt extract, and other grits or grains (rice, corn, oats, rye, etc.). These can be employed to supply extra starch for conversion and make subtle flavor changes. An economy is to substitute sugar in one form or another for some of the malt, but this process must not be carried too far.

If one is formulating a recipe, a sensible combination of malt, malt extract, grits, and sugar is probably the most easy, economical, and satisfactory solution.

Malt Quality

Only the best barley goes for malting purposes, and once it has been malted, it should be thin-skinned and float when put into water, and it should still be sweet in taste and smell.

Some malts on offer are of poor quality, but a good malt on mashing, at 1 lb. (450 g.) to 5 quarts (4.5 liters), could produce a wort with an OG of up to 1025 (a brewery might get twenty-five percent more).

Malt, like coffee, can be roasted light or dark, and is sold under various descriptions and in various forms. But the main fact to remember is the basic malt of all brewing, from which the strength of the beer is derived, is pale malt, simply because this gives the highest yield.

Generally speaking, the more a malt is roasted (i.e., the darker it is), the lower its yield. Thus pale malt is employed to obtain strength, while colored malts are added in small quantities to deepen color or alter flavor.

Colored malts are given various names, according to their depth of color. Thus one comes across crystal, amber, caramel, brown, and black malts. Crystal and caramel malts are kilned in the same way as pale malt, but afterward are roasted lightly and are therefore a deep golden color. They are excellent for adding body to sweeter beers. The content of the granule is crisp, and, used at 1 lb. (450 g.) per 5 quarts (4.5 liters), such a malt will give possibly 16 or 17 degrees of gravity, if mashing is carried out carefully. The yield is not so important as in the case of pale malt, of course, because these malts are likely to be used only to impart body or a more interesting color to the beer, and need not be more than a twentieth of the total quantity of malt used (that is the commercial level). Used in large quantities, they can convey a very pleasant, light, and nutty flavor, as in the best bitter beers.

Amber and brown malts are similar, but slightly darker, and give a slightly deeper tone in the finished beer. The granule's contents are more powdery. These malts are useful for lending a smooth full taste, which is useful in the case of mild or brown ales. They are not used so much these days.

Black malt has been much more heavily roasted, and at higher temperatures, so much so that it will give a wonderful depth of color. Its yield, however, in terms of gravity, will be low, probably not more than two or three degrees per pound per 5 quarts (450 g. per 4.5 liters). The roasting process is a delicate one, for if the temperature is too high the malt will be burned, but if it is too low it will not be caramelized. The temperature, therefore, has to be held between the two relevant levels (440°-480°F, 227°-249°C). Black malts give stout its burnt and rather woody taste, and in the case of sweet stouts, caramel is sometimes added to give the desired smoothness and sweetness. In a stout wort, the alcoholic strength, again, is derived from the pale malt, three parts of which will be used to each one part of black.

All of these malts, of course, have to be mashed by the home brewer to extract the flavor, but he can take a shortcut and avoid even this rather tricky job by employing malt extract. Generally, the principle to remember is: the more malt, the more body imparted finally to the drink. And the more body it has, the more it will need some bitter herb added to counteract the heaviness and keep the palate clear.

Roast barley is not so rich in flavor as black malt and gives a drier finish, so it is useful in, for instance, dry stouts. It is merely grain roasted to a reddish brown. It has not been malted.

Adjuncts

The starch in green malt is converted to sugar during mashing by the enzyme diastase. Diastase is sufficiently powerful to convert not only the starch of the malt, but that of any other grain (or grit) added to it. A malt or malt extract that has this ability to a great degree is described as highly diastatic. We can take advantage of this and reduce the cost—or increase the strength—of our brews by including in a formulation a proportion of other grits, such as flaked rice, flaked corn, flaked barley, or torrified barley, all of which must be cooled before use. Small quantities of these can be included in the boil-up when making extract beers, principally to effect flavor and color changes, but also making a contribution to the beer's strength. They are described in more detail in Chapter 11: True Beers.

There are other adjuncts such as torrified barley, wheat malt, wheat syrup, and various brewing flours that are most interesting to experiment with, but they are not generally readily available. Oats and rye, too, are rarely used.

Malt Extract

This the home brewer reconstitutes by the addition of water and hops, and the resultant wort can then be fermented like any other.

Some malt extracts are diastatic so that other starch grits can be used with them, and their starch converted by the diastase of the extract. And some are already hopped.

Sugars

In brewing, the term sugar has a special meaning, for it covers anything that can be a source of sugar, or starch, whether malt, barley, corn, rice, or sugar-producing ingredient, used in beer. Some of the sugar necessary in home brewing may come from malt (maltose), but sometimes it will be too expensive to obtain all the sugar necessary for a strong, or even a reasonably strong, brew in this way. Consequently, additional sugar will be needed. This can be added by means of ordinary white household sugar (sucrose), either cane or beet (chemically they are identical).

In Bavaria, incidentally, this is illegal, because German law recognizes beer only as a drink made from malt, hops, and water; no other sugar must be employed. This is not the case in breweries in many other countries, and the home brewer will certainly not wish to circumscribe himself in this way, when by adding extract or sugar, he can make beer far stronger than that normally on sale.

As a rough guide to the total amount of sugar to be used, one can say most beers will require between ½ lb. (250 g.) and 1 lb. (450 g.) of malt, or malt extract, and possibly, in addition, up to ¾ lb. (350 g.) of granulated sugar per 5 quarts (4.5 liters).

White sugar

Relatively small additions of white household sugar or sucrose for the purposes of economy will not affect the flavor of your brew, but too much sugar, rather than extract or malt, will produce a thin but over-strong beer, poor head retention—and probably a hangover. The higher the proportion of maltose and the lower the proportion of sucrose, the better the brew, in terms of flavor, body, and head retention. Household sugar is best used for pale light-bodied beers.

Darker sugars

Brown moist sugars, on the other hand, are excellent for darker beers, giving a distinctive roundness and character to them, and are therefore well worth the extra cost when these special characteristics are needed. In this category fall Light Brown, Soft Brown, Raw Brown, and Natural Brown sugars.

Invert sugar

This is added to brewery wort before it is hopped and boiled in order to increase its fermentability. It undoubtedly ferments quickest of all, but can be difficult to buy. When yeast sets to work on sucrose, it first splits it into its two main components, glucose and fructose, or inverts it, making a sugar that is then speedily fermentable. Thus, by using invert sugar, the fermentation is enabled to get away more speedily, because the yeast does not have first to effect the inversion.

If you use invert sugar (which is slightly more expensive than sucrose), note that because it contains more water it will be necessary to substitute 1.25 lb. (625 g.) for every 1 lb. (450 g.) of household sugar specified in recipes. It certainly makes a dry beer of real quality.

Invert sugar can be made quite easily as follows: Put 8 lb. (4 kg.) ordinary sugar (sucrose, i.e., cane or beet) in a large pan with 2 pints (1 liter) of water and half a heaping teaspoon of citric or tartaric acid. Heat this mixture until it boils, stirring occasionally with a wooden spoon until the sugar has been dissolved. Boil gently for half an hour or so, cool, and add about 2 pints (1 liter) of water to give a total volume of exactly 5 quarts (4.5 liters). One pint (500 ml.) of this syrup contains 1 lb. (450 g.) of invert sugar.

Glucose

Glucose is now available to the home brewer and is an ideal material, for it ferments well and quickly. Glucose is sold in the form of a fine white powder (dextrose monohydrate). It used to be sold cheaply as a soft lumpy brown material, known as glucose chips, but this form of glucose seems to have vanished from the market. Glucose will make a smooth and slightly dry beer.

Licorice

Licorice is an herb, is sweet to the taste, and can be useful for taking the harshness off a stout, but it should be avoided in finer beers, where it will spoil the clean taste. It does give the illusion of added body and sweetness, plus a peculiar pungency of its own, but all it has in fact done is to coat the tongue.

Caramel

This is the most commercial name for what used to be called burnt sugar, and is most useful in brewing as a general colorant. By its aid, brews can easily be tinted from a light brown to a really dark color, depending upon the quantity used. It can be purchased as gravy browning liquid, which sounds peculiar, but it will be seen from the label that this is in fact caramel. The amount to be used varies from a teaspoon in 15 quarts (13.5 liters) for bitter to 2 tablespoons for a dark brown, and it is added at the boiling stage.

Caramel can be made thus: Put a tablespoon of white sugar into half a pint (250 ml.) of water. Bring to boiling. Do not stir. Lower gas or heat and let syrup simmer till it turns to white candy, then stir slowly. The syrup will gradually turn a light brown color. Keep stirring until the caramel is nearly black. Then remove from gas and put on approximately half a pint (250 ml.) of cold water. Bring this slowly to the boil, stirring all the time until caramel is completely dissolved.

Lactose

Lactose, the milk sugar that is added to what was once called "milk stout" (the name is no longer used nowadays, because it was held to be misleading, implying the inclusion of milk in the beer), is not fermentable by usual brewing yeasts, and therefore, if used, will remain in the drink simply as sweetening. It can be added to a stout, or other beer, at the rate of 3-4 oz. to 5 quarts (90-120 g. to 4.5 liters). Lactose can be purchased from most chemists, but one needs to be careful to buy only the best quality. If it has an unduly cheesy flavor, reject it. Generally speaking, its use as a sweetener is not recommended.

Artificial sweeteners

Neither is the use of saccharin, which, after a while, breaks down and imparts bitterness, rather than sweetness, to the finished beer. Better for this purpose are sweeteners such as "Sweetex Liquid" or Sorbitol, used with great caution, a drop at a time. Aspartame sweeteners are also very effective, either as sold generally (Canderel, etc.), or as a stable solution, such as the Vinsweet distributed by VINA. These will not re-ferment.

Treacles and syrups

Treacles and syrups (molasses, black treacle, golden syrup, etc.) are best reserved for experimental purposes, their flavors being so unpredictable. Brown sugars are infinitely preferable.

It is the flowers of the hop that
we use in brewing.

Hops

The part that hops play in the production of quality beer is all-important, for
they affect flavor, condition, and keeping qualities.

The hop, with its delicate fresh flavor (when used in small amounts), is
the natural partner to malt. Its bitterness, even when strong, is never
disagreeable. Moreover, in an age of tranquillizers, it should be recognized as a
natural soporific (the hop pillow is an old remedy), and sleep comes easily after
hopped beer.

The chemistry of the hop and its influence on the brew is complicated, but it
is sufficient here to say that the hop contributes three main things: volatile oils,
giving aroma and flavor; resins, giving bitterness and improving the keeping
qualities of the beer; and tannin-like constituents, which make for brilliance.

Originally, hops were regarded mainly as a preservative, but nowadays their
flavoring function takes eminence, because the bitter flavor of hops has come to
be appreciated and expected in a beer. The bitterness of a brew can be adjusted
by increasing or decreasing the amount of hops used. The more hops, the more
bitter the finished drink. High quality pale ales and bitter beers are heavily
hopped, mild ales and stouts usually less so, and lagers least of all.

The type of hop chosen also governs the degree of bitterness. Of the three constituents, oils, resins, and tannins, it is one part of the resins, alpha acid, or humulon, that provides most of the bitterness and keeping qualities. Beta acid is also present, and in larger quantities, but has only a tenth of the bittering power, so it has become the practice to grade hops by their alpha acid content, those with high alpha acid being generally the most sought after.

Generally speaking ⅓-1 oz. (8.5-30 g.) of hops (the dried cones that carry the seeds of the female hop plant, *Humulus Lupulus*) are used to 5 quarts (4.5 liters), but exactly how much depends upon the type of hop and the type of beer being made. The higher the gravity, the more hops will be required.

Thus light ale, mild ale, and brown ale (all 1030-1035 SG) will require 0.4 oz. (11 g.) of hops per 5 quarts (4.5 liters), sweet stout and bitter (1035-1045 SG) will both need 0.5 oz. (15 g.), dry stout and pale ale (1040 SG) 0.7 oz. (20 g.), and barley wine (1060 SG) 1 oz. (30 g.) per 5 quarts (4.5 liters). Lager may require only .5 oz. per 5 quarts (15 g. per 4.5 liters).

There is little point in giving an exhaustive catalogue of hop varieties, because they will not all be generally available to the home brewer, so I list here only popular and widely used varieties. It may well be that even these will eventually be unavailable due to rapid changes in today's society. Most of the following are available:

Fuggle

Alpha acid 3.5-4.2%. A Kentish hop used for more than one hundred years that is probably still the favorite of the brewing industry. Strong-flavored, and therefore useful in the stronger-flavored beers such as mild and brown ales. Branding Cross (5-6%) is similar.

Golding

Alpha acid 3.5-5%. Named after a Kentish grower who established the strain over 160 years ago, this hop is lighter in flavor and is best used in light ales, best bitters, and beers of that type. Excellent for dry hopping if so desired. Whitbreads Goldings Varieties (WGV), 4.5-5%, are better.

Northern Brewer

Alpha acid 6-8%. A markedly bitter hop, so much so that 2 oz. (55 g.) is enough for 22.5-25 quarts (20-22.5 liters). Excellent in stouts.

Bullion

Alpha acid 4-9%. An American variety noted for its outstanding bitterness. Its strength of flavor is such that it can really only be used in conjunction with other hops, but is particularly valuable in stouts, or very bitter beers, and in long-maturing beers. Galena is another American hop with similar characteristics.

Hallertauer

Alpha acid 7-9%. A Bavarian hop that is now being imported and from which noble beers can be brewed. Particularly useful in light grain malt beers.

Saaz

Alpha acid 6-8%. Another imported hop that is ideal for the making of lager, because it has a delicate dry flavor and not too pronounced as an aroma.

Styrian Goldings

Alpha acid 6-8.5%. Despite their name, these hops are more like Fuggles in their characteristics. Very expensive.

Other varieties that may be encountered occasionally, or purchased from specialist suppliers include: Bramling, Cascade, Challenger, Concord, Mailing, Mount Hood, Northdown, Target. Whitbread Golding Variety (WGV), and Williamette.

Many brewers are tempted to try harvesting and drying wild hops, which are often to be found in the countryside, but this is usually an abortive exercise. Their inferiority and the impossibility of proper control during the drying process produces a poor quality dried hop, and that in turn means a low-grade beer. Do not be tempted, for the same reason, to buy cheap old compressed hops, which have probably lost most of their aroma.

Hop Pellets and Powders

It is useful to have such background knowledge about hops, and any keen brewer will profit by reading Dave Line's *Big Book of Brewing*, which goes into the subject in more detail.

It seems likely, however, that the use of whole hops may gradually become a thing of the past, for in the commercial world they are rapidly giving way to hop pellets, or processed hops in other forms. These have now been introduced into the homebrew trade, but do not seem to have replaced the whole hop cones, despite their convenience and unvarying quality. The only snag is they do not provide a natural filter bed like the whole hop, and can lead to cloudy beers unless used with care, and they are probably best employed in conjunction with ordinary hops. The pellets and powders are sold in sterile sealed sachets to protect their flavor and maximize their keeping qualities, and are well worth experimenting with, because they offer a quick road to good flavor.

Isomerized hop extracts are sold under various trade names, such as Hop Aroma, and are highly concentrated extracts of the essential hop oils and resins, obtainable in two or three strengths. They can be used to add additional flavor and aroma to a finished beer, and are very efficient indeed employed in this way, but owing to their extremely high concentration must be used with the utmost caution. A drop of the oil to 5 quarts (4.5 liters) is often sufficient. It is best added to a jug of the beer before bottling and then well stirred. The beer from the jug can then be returned to the bulk and well stirred.

Other Herbs

Although the hop is now preeminent, other herbs can be used to impart both flavor and bitterness, and for centuries were. It is well worthwhile to experiment with these alternate options, such as spruce oil. Spruce oil is also a good preservative (and combines well with hops), but, unlike hops, will dispel drowsiness rather than create it. Consequently, spruce beer, with its clean fresh flavor is a good refresher. It is still popular in Scandinavia. Nettles were once used in making stouts. An infusion of nettle is slightly salty (a requirement in stouts) and if nettle is used, it will need plenty of hops or the roughness of black malt to give it an edge and make it palatable. Salt gives beer, like coffee, a roundness of flavor, but as soon as the salty taste becomes perceptible, it is unpleasant, and the characteristic clean aftertaste of beer is lost. Other old-time flavorings include ginger, dandelion, burdock, and sarsaparilla. One can experiment with these to find stimulating variations upon the more usual hop theme. Once the principle of balancing sweetness against bitterness is understood, it becomes easy. It is worth trying some of these flavorings experimentally, if only to see just why the hop eventually won.

Water (or Liquor)

It is not accidental that the best beers in Britain are brewed at Burton-on-Trent, that Hampshire is famous for its bitter, or that Ireland, like London, is renowned for her stouts and porters, for the brewing of particular beers was once very much a matter of the composition of the water in the locality. High quality pale ales and bitter beers such as produced at Burton-on-Trent demand the type of water that occurs there naturally, water containing a comparatively high proportion of gypsum, or calcium sulfate. This helps one to attain clarity in the finished beer because it aids the separation of certain nitrogenous elements in the malt, which can be filtered off with the spent hops.

It has been said that to be ideal for bitters, such water should contain 21 grains per 5 quarts (4.5 liters) of calcium sulfate and 7 grains per 5 quarts (4.5 liters) of magnesium sulfate. Chlorides are not essential.

Mild ales and stouts and the best lagers, on the other hand, are made with soft water, often described as London type, containing a fair amount of calcium and magnesium carbonate and a certain amount of chlorides.

Generally, it will pay you to make the type of drink best made with your local water, soft or hard, and to ignore the niceties of water adjustment. Certainly that is the best plan if you are making kit beers. Far more important is to keep an eye on the quality of your water supply and, for instance, to avoid brewing on any occasion that it is noticeably chlorinated. If, however, you wish to progress to the real niceties of brewing, it will pay you to study Water Treatment in Chapter 10.

Yeast

Baker's yeast is not satisfactory for beer because it does not settle down into a firm sediment and will rise in clouds in the beer at the slightest movement of a barrel or bottle or when a screw stopper is removed. Racking is difficult and undue wastage is caused.

Most breweries have their own favorite strains of *Saccharomyces cerevisiae*, which do have some effect upon the character of their finished products. If you are lucky, you can sometimes obtain a jar from your local brewery. Such a yeast is naturally excellent for your purpose, for it will already have a pronounced beery flavor, and once you have some, if you are brewing weekly, you will always have an ample supply, and probably an almost embarrassing surplus. I once kept one such brewery yeast continually in use for over two years. At that time, I was brewing weekly in glass jars, and all that was necessary, after racking one brew into 2.5-quart (2 liter) bottles, was to throw out two-thirds of the lees, leaving just sufficient to fill the peripheral groove at the bottom of the jar. The new wort was then siphoned in on top of this and fermentation would begin immediately.

There is always an active yeast sediment in real ale, so if you are on sufficiently good terms with the landlord at your local bar, he may be persuaded to let you have a half pint (250 ml.) or so from the bottom of a cask for you to culture onward.

You can also make a starter bottle from the dregs of a bottle of certain bottled beers. Allow the bottle to stand undisturbed for two or three days, then pour off your drinks, leaving a couple of inches of beer behind, containing any yeast that may be in that particular bottle. Make up a solution of ¼ pint (120 ml.) of hot water, 1 teaspoon of sugar, 1 teaspoon of malt extract, and a lump of citric acid the size of a pea. When this is cool, pour it into the beer bottle, plug it with cotton wool, and stand it in a warm place, such as the airing cupboard. If you are lucky (it depends largely on what type of beer or stout you are using) you will get a vigorous fermentation that can be used as a starter for your next brew. Several of the better-known bottled beers can be used in this way. Guinness is now pasteurized, but one that is rarely found to fail is Worthington White Label. The dregs of a bottle of home brew, of course, make an excellent starter for a following brew because there is much more yeast sediment in a bottle of home brew than in a bottle of commercial beer. So once you have acquired a tiny amount of true brewer's yeast, you need never be without ample supplies. Indeed, you are eventually likely to have so much that you will be throwing quantities away every time you bottle.

Brewery yeasts, it should be noted, are usually top-fermenting varieties. This often involves some skimming, for a thick cake of yeast will form and float on the surface of the beer. I find that the particular top yeast I most commonly use produces a real mat of yeast on the surface of the beer, so much so that skimming is necessary every two days or so.

The initial scum and surplus yeast should be skimmed off, but once a creamy foam appears—the so-called cauliflower head or rocky head—do not skim again until you are going to bottle. A few teaspoons of yeast from the lees of a brew can also be used.

Such surplus yeast, of course, provides an excellent starter for the next brew, but there is always far too much, and quantities have to be thrown away.

Yeast will keep about a week in the wet state. Take a few spoonfuls from the pancake of floating yeast, or from the lees, and dry them off on clean blotting paper or cloth. Then mold the yeast into a knob, put it into a polythene bag or glass jar with loose-fitting lid, and pop it into the fridge until wanted.

Most brewers, we believe, will at first plump for a reliable granular yeast such as those sold by homebrew shops in sachets or tubs and are quite satisfactory, if not quite as good, as a wet yeast from a brewery. Use about a heaping teaspoon to 5 quarts (4.5 liters).

Lager yeasts (which are bottom, not top, fermenters) are excellent. They do settle firmly, allowing the clear beer to be racked off easily.

There is little point in using a nutrient with the yeast as one does in winemaking, for malt extract is itself a superb nutrient. In cases of sluggish fermentations or where fermentation is slow to start, however, it may be useful to add a proprietary yeast energizer and/or a good pinch of citric acid to a 25-quart (22.5 liter) brew. That is enough to give the trace of acidity that yeast likes without affecting the flavor.

Use a flour sieve to skim scum and surplus yeast off the fermenting beer.

CHAPTER 9

EQUIPMENT YOU WILL NEED

Because beer, obviously, is drunk in larger quantities than wine, by the pint or half-pint (250-500 ml.), one naturally tends to brew in greater bulk. While one can still make experimental single gallons (4 liters), most home brewers eventually come round to the idea of making 20 or 25 quarts (18-22.5 liters) at a time. This is about the largest quantity that a man can comfortably lift.

Making a List

For boiling

Most kit beers do not demand the use of a large boiler, and you may well be able to manage with a large 7.5- or 10-quart (7.5-9 liter) saucepan in which you can boil sufficient water to dissolve the extract, adding the remainder cold.

It will not be long, however, before you start thinking of equipment yourself to brew in a rather more sophisticated fashion, and if you intend attempting mashed beers, you will certainly need to do so, because you will need to be able to boil and handle larger quantities.

If you have a large boiler to sit on a gas stove, such as a 20- or 25-quart (18-22.5 liter) aluminum one, or even a 15-quart (13.5 liter) "dixie" such as I used for some years, you will find it useful, but there is no doubt that in the long run the ideal solution is an electric or gas boiler holding about 35 quarts (32 liters). It is certainly necessary if you are making beers other than from home kits. I use a purpose-designed Bruheat boiler, which is perfect for the job, and which can be obtained from homebrew shops. It is a large polypropylene bucket fitted with an electric element and controlled by a sensitive thermostat that has a range between 50°F and 212°F (10°C and 100°C) and thus can cope

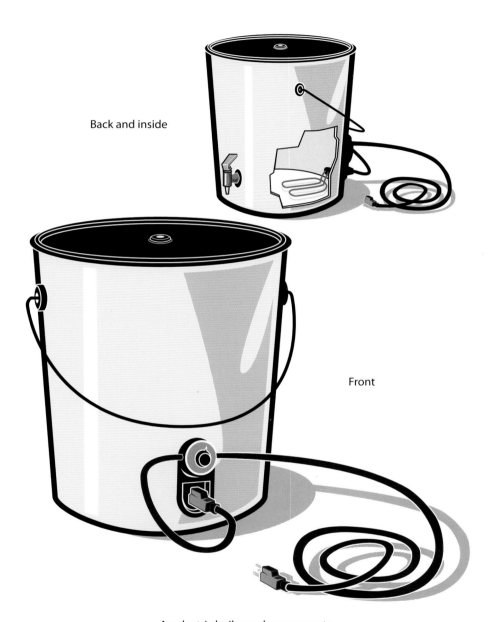

Back and inside

Front

An electric boiler and components

with all three processes involved: mashing, boiling, and fermenting. The Thorne Electrim is similar.

Iron or galvanized boilers, incidentally, are safe enough for water or for boiling up a mash, but must not be used if there is any acid whatsoever in the formulation, because there may be a risk of metal poisoning.

For infusing

For infusing hops, a large bag of nylon mesh with a string for easy removal is useful. The hops can be boiled in this and are easily removed before fermenting begins. You can either make a bag yourself or buy one at a homebrew shop.

For mashing

When making a beer or stout from malt or other grain there are two main methods you can follow. You can mash the grain in a large saucepan, or in a polythene bucket with immersion heater, and then sparge into your boiler, straining the grain in a stout bag with a mesh bottom inside your boiler. Or you can mash in the bag in the electric boiler, using part of your wort.

If you use a 10-quart (9 liter) polythene bucket, you will also need a 50-watt immersion heater, with or without thermostat. And a thermometer is indispensable.

Electric boiler, strainers, straining and sparging bags, polypropylene spoon

Straining and Sparging Bags

For fermenting

For fermenting and general brewing uses, the best buy is undoubtedly a white plastic "brewbin" holding about 30 quarts (27 liters), to be obtained from homebrew shops, or the chemist's. Made of food-grade white polystyrene, such bins are safe, light, easy-to-clean, and a joy to use, and they have an airtight lid to which a fermentation lock can be fitted if desired. They are fairly inexpensive and are virtually essential. It is particularly helpful if your bin is graduated in gallons and liters either inside or out, and is translucent so that you can see how much it contains. This is useful when handling large quantities of liquid.

Do not be tempted to use the many non-homebrew containers that are available cheaply or even free, which are made of colored plastic, or have been used for strange substances like dog shampoo, putty, or emulsion paint. Colored plastics often contain dangerous chemicals, such as chrome and cobalt, and may be made from recycled scrap plastic. Secondhand containers may well have been impregnated with oils and chemicals, flavors that can't be got rid of—yes, plastics are absorbent—and should be avoided. What you are making is a good health-giving brew, and it is unwise to ferment it in anything but food-grade containers made from virgin white plastic. And this container will become your primary fermenter. If the ambient temperature is low, it can help to stand your fermenter on an electric heating tray, or place a heating belt around it. Whichever you use, this becomes your primary fermenter.

A range of fermenters

For measuring

Do not fiddle about in beer brewing with 1-pint (500 ml.) measures. A 5-quart (4.5 liter) glass jar or saucepan will save a lot of time, as will marking out quantities on your brewbin. But make sure your jar does hold 8 pints, 4 liters, (some hold more, some less) and then reserve it for that purpose.

For straining

Straining of small quantities is best done with a large nylon flour sieve, easy to use and clean, but if you are dealing regularly with big quantities of hops, and grain or bran, it will pay you to make a wooden "picture-frame" crisscrossed by tape or cord, to fit the top of your vessel. Or use a garden sieve. On this it is then a simple plan to lay a piece of muslin, and the whole mash can be tipped out in one go and left to drain, instead of having to be strained a little at a time.

For siphoning

Make yourself a siphon from 5 or 6 feet (1.5-2 meters) of transparent acrylic tubing. You can either fit it with a glass or stainless steel J-tube at the intake end (so that it draws clear beer down from above and does not suck up sediment) or fit it with a float as illustrated. Use a thick 8-in. (20 cm.) disc or square of wood and push the end of the tube through a hole in the middle so that it projects slightly underneath. Some 1-in. (2.5 cm.) dowel legs glued and screwed underneath prevent any great disturbance or pickup of sediment.

For 'resting' your beer

It is advisable to let your beer rest for a week before bottling or kegging it, but it must be protected from any air-borne contamination. It is a good idea to have a spare fermenter, or a bin with a tightly-fitting lid, with a plastic tap near the base. Rack the beer into this, and let it stand for a few days. The tap makes it much easier to control the flow of beer when bottling and ensures the slight sediment is not disturbed.

For easy handling

Make yourself a trolley from a rectangle of 0.5-in. (about 1 cm.) wood—I used marine ply—with a strong castor fixed under each corner, so that it stands 2-3 in. high (5-7.5 cm.). Your brewbin, or primary fermenter, stands on this, and the wort can easily be run into it from your boiler's tap. Such a trolley makes it possible to move a 25-quart, 22.5-liter (or even bigger) brew with ease.

A trolley like this takes away a lot of the hard work.

For water in quantity

I have also found it extremely useful when handling these large containers (which are too big to fit under the tap in many kitchen sinks) to have a 4-foot (just over 1 meter) domestic hose, which fits onto the mixer tap and which has a rigid piece of tubing to give a smooth jet at the delivery end. This makes washing out, rinsing, and filling of large containers with either hot or cold water much easier.

For bottling

For bottling your beer, you will need to collect or buy beer or cider bottles of thick strong glass, capable of withstanding the 30 lb. p.s.i. (13.5 kg.) pressure that will be generated inside them. Wine bottles, spirit bottles, and any bottle not designed to stand up to such pressure are lethal. Brown polyethylene terephthalate (PET) plastic bottles, used commercially, are acceptable.

You will need enough containers to hold 20 or 25 quarts (18-22.5 liters) at a time. You can either retain them when you buy bottled beer or purchase a couple of dozen outright at an off-license, public house, or homebrew shop. Reject any that are cracked, or that have chips around the neck or base, making the bottle weak at that point and leading to a risk of its exploding as pressure builds up within it. Discard all one-trip non-returnable bottles.

Suitable bottles, mallet and cappers, various crown caps, seals, and stoppers

Nowadays, you are most likely to come across bottles that have to be sealed by special tin crown caps. These can be obtained quite cheaply from homebrew shops and are easily crimped onto the bottles using a simple tool, giving your bottle a truly professional air. One can also buy push-on plastic closures such as continentals use for wine bottles and some breweries now use to re-seal crown-closed bottles. Swing-top resealable bottles are also easy to use.

You may be fortunate enough still to come across some of the screw-stoppered flagons that were once in common use. If so, grab them, because although they are perfect for our purpose, they are fast becoming obsolete. They are economic to use because the stoppers can be sterilized and used over and again. Check that the rubber rings are not perished or missing. If they are, your beer will go flat. If any show defects, obtain replacements.

For bottle cleaning

Wire-handled bottle-cleaning brushes are useful. An even more handy idea is a cube cut from a nylon scouring pad and fixed with glue or wire to the end of an 18-in. (46 cm.) dowel.

For checking gravity: the hydrometer

The hydrometer, like the thermometer, will enable you to brew with precision.

The beer hydrometer (usually graduated 1000-1100) will tell you the gravity of your wort, the strength of your beer, and most importantly, when it is safe to bottle. Most beers have starting gravities between 1010 and 1060, as will be seen on the table on the next page, and must on no account be bottled if the final gravity is above 1010.

A hydrometer in use

Typical starting gravities of commercial beers are (sugar in the table below means sugar and/or malt):

Type of Brew	SG	Potential % alcohol by vol.	Amount of sugar in the liquid		Amount of sugar added to the liquid		Vol. with sugar added			
			US	Metric	US	Metric	US		Metric	
			lb.	oz	g.	lb.	oz.	g.	qt.	fl. oz.	liters	ml.
	1010	0.9	-	2	56	-	2.5	71	5	1	4.5	30
	1015	1.6	-	4	113	-	5	142	5	3	4.5	89
	1020	2.3	-	7	198	-	8	227	5	5	4.5	148
	1025	3.0	-	9	255	-	10	283	5	7	4.5	207
Mild, light, lager	1030	3.7	1	12	340	-	13	368	5	8	4.5	237
Pale ale, bottled	1035	4.4	1	15	425	1	0	450	5	10	4.5	296
Pale ale, porter	1040	5.1	1	1	482	1	2	510	5	11	4.5	325
Strong ales, stout	1045	5.8	1	3	539	1	4	567	5	13	4.5	384
Strong ales, stout	1050	6.5	1	5	595	1	7	652	5	14	4.5	414
Extra stout	1055	7.2	1	7	652	1	9	709	5	16	4.5	473
Very strong ales	1060	7.8	1	9	709	1	11	765	5	17	4.5	503
Very strong ales	1065	8.6	1	11	765	1	14	850	5	19	4.5	562
Very strong ales	1070	9.2	1	13	822	2	1	935	5	20	4.5	591

Subtract the final gravity from the initial gravity and divide the answer by 7.36. That is the strength of your beer in terms of percentage alcohol by volume.

It is interesting to compare the strengths in the third column above with those of other drinks, e.g., claret, 9.7%; Chateauneuf du Pape, 12.5%; champagne, 13.5%; sherry, 18.9%; port, 20.2%; and whisky, 40%.

Do not forget that hydrometers are designed to be read when the liquid is at 59°F (15°C), and if it is at any other temperature, you should allow for it as in the following table. Omit the decimal point of the specific gravity and make the correction to the resulting number.

Example: A hydrometer reading of 1140 at 86°F should be corrected to 1143.4.

Temperature		Correction
°C	°F	
10	50	Subtract 0.6
15	59	Correct
20	68	Add 0.9
25	77	Add 2
30	86	Add 3.4
35	95	Add 5
40	104	Add 6.8

A typical record of the progress of a fermentation:

Initial SG of wort before adding yeast (also referred to as OG)	1040
SG after 1 day	1034
SG after 2 days	1023
SG after 3 days	1011
SG after 4 days	1006
SG after 5 days	1003
SG after 6 days	1001
SG after 7 days	1000

Other useful equipment

From this you will see that a highly efficient setup capable of regularly brewing 25 quarts (22.5 liters) at a time would include:

- Bruheat or other large electric boiler
- 30-quart (27 liter) brewbin, with lid
- One or two 25-quart (22.5 liter) containers or spare pressure barrel
- Siphon
- Beer hydrometer and jar
- Thermometer (32°-212°F, 0°-100°C)
- 25-quart (22.5 liter) pressure barrel, preferably with injector

Or

- Sufficient beer bottles
- A large nylon or polypropylene spoon or paddle

In addition to this, you will need things probably already in the kitchen: scales, measures, kitchen spoons, a ¹⁄₁₀ oz. (5 ml.) measuring spoon, a large sieve or strainer, and, if bottling, a bottlebrush, a small funnel, crown caps, and a capping tool.

All the equipment needed to produce a successful at-home brew

CHAPTER 10

BREWING TECHNIQUES

Whichever way you are making your beer, certain essential processes are likely to be involved, such as:

a) Adjusting the water quality, if necessary

b) Boiling the wort

c) Fermenting

d) Racking off and "resting"

e) Fining

f) Bottling or barreling

g) Carbonating

Water Treatment

Water treatment for brewing purposes is a complicated subject, and if you wish to go in for competitive brewing it would be as well to study it further. Most home brewers, however, will find it sufficient just to ascertain from their local water company the exact composition of their own supply.

This is a terrifyingly detailed document, but the only factor with which you need concern yourself is the total hardness. (Hardness is subdivided into "temporary" and "permanent," temporary hardness being that which is removed by boiling. Total hardness is sometimes given in parts per million (milligrams per liter) and sometimes as Clarke's Degrees, and waters are classified, using these scales, as follows:

Total Hardness		Water Type
p.p.m., mgm./liter	Clarke's Degrees	
0-100	0-7	Soft
100-200	7-14	Medium Soft
200-400	14-28	Moderately Hard
400-600	28-42	Hard
More than 600	More than 42	Very Hard

It is sufficient for our purpose to distinguish between soft and hard. You probably know quite well which your water is, but if you do not, just boil 5 quarts (4.5 liters) of water for twenty minutes or so, let it cool, and see if it leaves a chalk deposit. If it does, the water is hard. Those who have lived in a hard water district will recognize this phenomenon in their pots.

Once you know whether your water is hard or soft you can easily adjust it for various brews.

Use a $\frac{1}{10}$ oz. (5 ml.) medicinal teaspoon as measure. I have used the common name of the substances, but if you have to order them from a chemist they are: Gypsum (calcium sulfate), Epsom salts (magnesium sulfate), chalk (calcium carbonate), and salt (sodium chloride). Adjust as follows:

Treatment for 25 quarts of hard water (22.5 liters)	
Bitter, Light and Pale Ales, Strong Ale, Barley Wine	Add 1 teaspoon flaked calcium chloride OR boil for fifteen minutes, siphon off, and add 1 teaspoon gypsum and ½ teaspoon Epsom salts.
Mild Ale, Brown Ale, Stout (sweet)	Add 1 teaspoon flaked calcium chloride OR boil for fifteen minutes, cool, siphon off, and add ½ teaspoon salt.
Irish stout (dry)	No treatment required.
Lager	Add 1 teaspoon flaked calcium chloride OR boil for fifteen minutes, cool, and siphon off.

Treatment for 25 quarts of soft water (22.5 liters)	
Bitter, Light and Pale Ales, Strong Ale, Barley Wine	Add 1 teaspoon gypsum and ½ teaspoon Epsom salts.
Mild Ale, ', Stout (sweet)	Add ½ teaspoon salt
Lager	No treatment required.

You can purchase in homebrew shops "water treatments" for different types of beer; you simply need to make sure you have the right one for your water and for the beer you intend making. It is also advisable to filter or boil all your brewing water to dispel the chlorine, as this can give an unpleasant taste like disinfectant.

Boiling

Boiling is necessary for several reasons, but principally to ensure that the wort is sterilized, to extract flavor from any loose hops employed, and, particularly with mashed beers, to achieve a hot break, or clarification by causing the flocculation of protein matter in suspension.

In the case of grain beers and mashed beers, the wort must be boiled for at least three-quarters of an hour, and preferably three-quarters more in order to achieve this hot break. And it is not sufficient just to simmer. It must be a good rolling boil. Eventually, the beer will clear, and if a glassful is removed, it will be seen that the proteins in suspension are clumping together in little lumps about the size of a match head and settling. When this occurs, you have achieved the hot break, but if when you test, the solids are still minute and in cloudy suspension, more boiling is necessary. Irish moss may be added during the last quarter of an hour to speed the process.

A point to note is that boiling also progressively darkens the wort, and therefore the finished beer. Half an hour will give a pale beer, but less will give an anemic looking one (quite apart from the fact that the wort will not be stabilized). Up to one and a half hours will produce a proportionately darker beer. For stout and extra stout, of course, black malt should be used to achieve that depth of color.

Some recipes reduce the boiling period to a minimum (this is obviously an attraction to the beginner), but it is really a mistake, and it is preferable, if the smell and steam from your brewery cause objections from the distaff side, to use an electric boiler on an extension cord in the garage, or even outdoors.

Ample boiling time is important if you are to obtain beers of quality, you will find.

Sterilization is achieved quite rapidly, but it is important to allow sufficient time for the full extraction of the flavor and aroma of any hops used, and this usually means at least three-quarters of an hour. So, for most beers, on all counts, hop flavor extraction, quality, and clarity, an hour's good rolling boil is usually adequate.

Pitching the Yeast

Fermentation takes place initially in a brewbin or plastic bag into which the wort is strained to leave behind any hops or grain. The yeast cannot be pitched (added) until the temperature has dropped to 60°F (15.5°C) and if your time is likely to be short, it is as well to make provision for the forced cooling of the wort by standing the boiler in a bath or sink of cold water or, if it is an electric one, to run a coil of hose through it from the cold water tap.

With dried yeasts, it helps the fermentation to get away to a good start if the yeast is rehydrated beforehand. This is simply done by sprinkling the yeast into two-thirds of a cup of lukewarm water and leaving it covered for fifteen or twenty minutes. Then stir it, and pitch in the usual way. Do not pitch the yeast until the wort is tepid or the yeast may be killed.

Help the fermentation to start by rehydrating any dry yeast you are using.

Fermentation

Fermentation will soon be vigorous as the yeast starts to consume the sugar in the wort, but it will be assisted if the wort is given a good rousing. Stir it vigorously with a large plastic spoon or paddle to get some oxygen into it before covering the bin with a cloth and then lightly replacing the lid. If using a bag, lightly tie the neck.

Keep the bin in a reasonably warm, but not hot, place (60°-70°F, 16°-21°C) and try to keep the temperature constant, because this will assist a steady fermentation. Most houses nowadays have a spot where a brew can be kept at a satisfactory temperature—a few degrees are not critical—and that of a centrally heated house is almost certainly right.

If necessary, a suitable temperature can be maintained by standing the fermenting bin on an electric heating tray, such as the Thome Electrim, or wrapping it with an electrical belt like the Brewmaker Brewbelt.

A frothy mass of foam will soon build up on the surface with some blobs of impurities, which will adhere to the inside of the bin round the edge of the surface. Skim these off, together with the initial head that forms, to be gradually replaced (if you are using a good top-fermenting yeast) by a thick pancake of floating yeast. This does tend to cut off the oxygen supply to the wort, and it pays, with such a top-fermenting yeast, to admit some air to the brew and also to agitate the "pancake" gently from below to keep live yeast circulating and without taking the dead yeast cells down into the brew. These yeasts ferment downward, as it were. If such fermentation is kept closely covered, the beer tends to acquire a rather sour taste.

As the fermentation gets underway, you will see a collection of yeast, called a yeast pancake, begin to form and float on the top of the beer.

If you are using bottom-fermenting yeast as when brewing lager, the foregoing does not apply, and the brew can be kept more closely covered.

Strong beers will normally ferment out in a week to ten days, weaker ones in three to five days.

Racking and Resting

Many recipes and kits advocate bottling or casking the beer direct from the primary fermenter, and this can be done as long as the SG is below 1010 and preferably down to 1005. Bottling sooner may lead to burst bottles.

The snag with this direct bottling is that it usually results in too much yeast finishing up in the bottles. It is infinitely preferable to allow the beer to rest for six to seven days in a 25-quart (22.5 liter) container under an air lock, before priming and bottling.

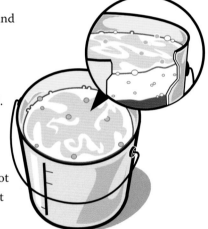

When fermentation is finished, rack (siphon) your beer into the container, being careful to leave all the yeast sediment behind. Add any finings, and fit airlock as explained hereafter, where the container requires it. There is a larger-than-normal hobby-type airlock suitable for beer-making, as it does not blow dry as rapidly as the smaller ones meant for 5-quart (4.5 liter) demijohns.

A head building up

Fining

Finings can be added at this stage if desired. You can buy proprietary dry beer finings (which are usually gelatin) or buy gelatin in half-ounce (15 g.) sachets. Heat half a pint (250 ml.) of water and stir the gelatin into it, but do not let it boil. Then add it to the racked beer and stir or agitate the beer vigorously to mix the finings thoroughly with it. I find it helpful to have the finings ready before starting siphoning and to add a portion of them to successive gallons so that they are fairly evenly distributed.

Isinglass, sold as liquid beer finings, is much more sensitive to temperature and much more difficult to use, and I do not recommend it for that reason.

You must, of course, have either an airlock or other means of allowing pressure to escape.

The beer can be left to be dealt with at your leisure for days or even two or three weeks. A week's rest is usually enough, the great advantage being that more yeast can settle out, and the finings can render the beer star bright. The end result is that one has just a paint coat of yeast in the bottle instead of a thick layer.

Siphon your beer from the fermentation bucket into a secondary vessel if you do not want to bottle it right away.

Priming

However you store your beer, in bottles or in kegs, it must first be primed if it is to have that so desirable head and sparkle. This, of course, is brought about by a further brief fermentation in bottle or keg. To achieve this, the beer will need to be "primed" after its rest with a little carefully-measured dose of sugar.

Priming the bottles

But first, test your beer with a hydrometer to ensure its SG is below 1010, and preferably 1005, or there may be too much sugar still present, in which case you will get a dangerous buildup of pressure in your bottles.

Priming sugar needs to be added at the rate of half a teaspoon per pint (500 ml.) or one level teaspoon per quart (1 liter). Do not exceed this dose, or you may have a Vesuvius when you open the bottle, or even a burst bottle.

For priming beer in bulk use equivalent amounts, 3 oz. to 25 quarts (90 g. to 22.5 liters). (If you propose using an injector to serve the beer by pressure, this can be reduced to 2 oz., 55 g.)

Filling the bottles

Bottling

When you have collected your bottles, wash and sterilize them thoroughly and then funnel the exact amount of priming sugar into each one, half a teaspoon for pints (500 ml.), 1 level teaspoon for quarts (1 liter). Work methodically, moving your funnel from bottle to bottle, so as to be sure that you do not double-dose any bottle by mistake.

Then siphon the beer into the bottles, letting it run gently down their sides to minimize foaming, and try to leave ¾ in. to 1 in. (2.5 cm.) air space below the stopper or closure to provide expansion room to absorb some of the pressure that will be created.

Most beers, despite having been rested, will still carry traces of yeast in suspension, sufficient to attack the fresh sugar and bring about in-bottle fermentation.

Crown-capping the bottles

If you wish to make sure, however, add a tiny quantity of fresh yeast, say two small shots per bottle.

Then seal your bottles with crown corks or screw stoppers, using one of the splendid tools now available, and, if you wish, label them to increase their professional appearance.

It is useful, too, to devise some color code for various types of brew—bitter, stout, lager, etc. This is most easily done by using the various colors of crown caps that one can buy.

Keep the bottles in a warm room for two or three days to encourage the fermentation, then move into a cool place, such as a larder, to assist clarification.

Do not drink your beer right away. It will need at least two weeks in the bottle to be drinkable and will improve for a month or so. Clarity, bead (the tiny bubbles), head, and flavor will all improve with true maturity, and it may well be months before the beer really goes "over the hill" and its flavor starts to deteriorate.

If beer is well chilled, it can often be rebottled without too much loss of gas, enabling you to pour a beer clear to the last drop. Whether you are prepared to go to this trouble depends on how fussy you are, I suppose. With home brew so cheap, most brewers feel they can afford to waste the last little bit clouded by sediment.

But generally this is unnecessary. If you feel so very aesthetic, it is far easier to use a pewter tankard. The beer will taste better and what the eye does not see...

Draught Beers

Partly because many brewers tire of endless bottle washing and partly because of the difficulties of obtaining a sediment-free beer in a bottle, the modern trend is away from bottling in favor of the pressurized container. There is nothing so satisfying as to be able to draw off a pint of your own.

Homebrew kegs

Several firms are now selling 5-quart (about 5 liter) steel kegs that can be filled with clear beer or lager and sealed with a rubber bung with a plastic core. Beer can be dispensed from these by using a small air pump, hand-operated, or by gas pressure dispensers from carbon dioxide bulbs. The plastic cores are driven into the keg when the tapping equipment is attached, and are recovered and reusable when the keg has been emptied. These kegs are easily portable, and are small enough to be chilled in the family refrigerator—excellent for lagers in particular.

Pressure barrels

With beer in a barrel, keg, or pipkin, the lees are left at the bottom and clear beer is drawn off from above them. This way of dispensing beer has become much more popular nowadays because one can buy a variety of devices for pressurizing barrels and kegs. The beer can be served under carbon dioxide pressure and no air need be admitted to the barrel, so that the beer will keep almost indefinitely. This is a big advantage. The only disadvantage is that beer takes much longer to clear in a cask or keg than it does in a bottle, because the

Homebrew kegs are a simple and easy storage solution for home brewers who want quick and easy access to their beer.

yeast has further to fall, so fining with isinglass or gelatin is to be advocated, or using a barrel fitted with a float take-off.

To do this, one needs a strong pressure-resistant plastic barrel or keg—there are a dozen or so makes available—and it is a good idea to invest in a carbon dioxide gas injection device to go with it to enable the beer to be dispensed to the last drop without contact with air.

Do not fiddle with old-fashioned wooden beer barrels. They are difficult to maintain in good condition, and the beer will almost certainly be flat before you can drink it all.

Of the custom-designed plastic barrels on the market, several have now stood the test of time and you can safely invest in, say, a Hambleton Bard Super-Cask or Beersphere, a Saffron Superkeg or Rotokeg, or any of the Weltonhurst range of barrels as supplied to the trade. You can also use a Drafty Five, a polypin specially designed for home brewers, incorporating a safety valve, if you can find one. Ritchie Products' Piggy is a horizontal pressure barrel, with a 4-in. (10 cm.) top aperture (please note that updated options have become available since this book was first published).

Homebrew kegs with carbon dioxide injectors and float take-offs make it possible to draw off the last drop of beer above the yeast sediment.

Injectors

If you intend dispensing the beer by natural pressure, you need to prime the bulk at the rate of 3 oz. of sugar to 25 quarts (90 g. to 22.5 liters). The first few pints will draw splendidly, but eventually you will have to admit air from the top and you are likely to run into difficulty in keeping a head on the last few pints (unless you can dispose of 20 quarts (18 liters) at one sitting, which is by no means unknown in home brewing circles).

Consequently, most brewers prefer to reduce the priming sugar to 2 oz. (55 g.), and back up the gas generated therefrom with a carbon dioxide gas injector using cartridges or cylinders. These are not called into operation until the natural pressure is exhausted, then the barrel can be given a quick squirt of gas from the injector, pressure is restored and, what is more, the beer is still protected from contact with air.

There are now many types of injectors and taps on the market, all of them with individual advantages, and which one you use is largely a matter of personal preference. Generally, those using larger cylinders of gas are preferable. Most common are Hambleton Bard's S20 and S30 cylinders, and Sodastream cylinders used with an adaptor (updated options available). They may be dearer to buy initially, but are much cheaper to run, because one cylinder can do the work of 30 bulbs, at least halving the cost of the actual gas. Another system has been developed by Widget World (Cryoservice Ltd. of Worcester), which can incorporate an adjustable reducing valve, so that with ordinary plastic tubing, one gas cylinder can be used to maintain gas pressure in several barrels if desired.

Your local homebrew shop can usually demonstrate the various types available and advise you in your choice.

CHAPTER 11

TRUE BEERS

Experienced home brewers are in little doubt that to obtain the highest-quality true beer one must do as the commercial brewery does and employ grain malt and the mashing process. Mashing consists of soaking the green malt in hot water and converting its starch to fermentable sugar, maltose.

It is significant that in almost all of the beer competitions that take place at the national and regional level, it is mashed grain beers that feature prominently in the prize lists, beers made almost entirely from malt, grain, and hops, with no added sugar.

(Anyone who is fortunate enough to have a vacation in Bavaria and has an opportunity of sampling the beers there, where the use of sugar is forbidden by law, will appreciate what a true malt and hops aroma should be.)

Any home brewer worth his salt will certainly want to try his hand at true beers, even if he does frequently, for convenience, turn to the employment of malt extract or brew from kits.

Some home brewers go so far as to try malting their own barley, but it is a tricky process and the chances of success are extremely small. It is far better to find a reliable supplier and purchase good-quality, ready-kilned malt, remembering that the bulk of the malt you will use should be pale malt, and that other malts are required mainly only for coloring and flavor changes. In mild and brown beers, they will be used in quite small proportions and at the most, as when making a stout, will only be a quarter of the total malt used. The really dark malts contribute hardly any sugar at all.

Devising Recipes

When devising one's own recipes using grain malt, it is essential to know how much maltose is likely to be obtained from any particular batch, because malts can vary enormously. This, if one is using a mixture of grains, can be somewhat complicated, because a series of tests and a proportion calculation will be required. The simplest plan is to work on the basis that the bulk of the malt used will be pale malt—as it will—and ignore the contribution to specific gravity made by the small amounts of other grain malts.

Good pale malt will yield four-fifths of its own weight as sugar, others less.

One does certainly need to assess the potential of the pale malt, and it is simplest to do this to arrive at a result in terms of the gravity produced by the use of 1 lb. (450 g.) of malt per 5 quarts (4.5 liters). Having discovered this, it is a matter of simple multiplication to decide how much malt per 5 quarts one needs to use to arrive at any desired original gravity.

Malt test

A simple test will obviate wasting hours of time in perhaps fruitless mashing. Take 2 oz. (55 g.) of your crushed pale malt and put it into a saucepan. Add half a pint (250 ml.) of water heated to 155°F (68°C), and hold the temperature as nearly as possible at 150°F (65°C) for an hour. Add a further half pint (250 ml.) of water at the same temperature and then allow to cool to just above 60°F (16°C). Strain through a coarse filter and check the specific gravity with your hydrometer. This will give the gravity resulting from the use of 1 lb. (450 g.) of that particular malt to 5 quarts (4.5 liters). If your test, for instance, produces a gravity of 1030, each ounce (30 g.) contributes roughly 2 degrees of gravity (30 ÷ 16). From this it is easy to calculate how much malt will be required to be certain of reaching the gravity you desire. Any malt, incidentally, that produces a gravity of less than 1023 in this test, is not really worth using.

Pale malt

It is important to purchase malt of the highest possible quality, clean and free of dust and rubbish, and with good plump grains of uniform size so that they will crush easily. The inside should be white and powdery if you crack it open and should taste distinctly of malt if bitten. Good pale malt has a light golden or straw color. Lager malt is the continental equivalent, but not so good.

Pale malts and some malt extracts are diastatic, that is to say they can convert to sugar the starch in any other grain mashed with them. Some can convert as much as a third of their own weight. But the more heavily malt is kilned (i.e., the darker it is), the more its diastatic ability is damaged. Heavily roasted or black malts have none at all, and all of their enzymes have been destroyed. They therefore contribute no sugar or conversion power to the mashing process.

If you locate a good pale malt, buy as much as you can afford, for it keeps well and it is always advisable to make a trial brew with a small quantity first.

Darker malts

As already explained, one can buy various darker malts, which are employed either to obtain darker beers or to effect subtle flavor changes.

Other grits and adjuncts

The starch in green malt is converted to sugar during mashing by the enzyme diastase. Diastase is sufficiently powerful to convert not only the starch of the malt, but that of any other grain (or grit) that is added to it. Malt that has this ability to a great degree is described as highly diastatic. We can take advantage of this and reduce the cost—or increase the strength—of our brews by including in the mash a proportion of other grains, or grits as they are called in commercial brewing, such as corn, oats, rice, or wheat. They are best employed to make subtle flavor changes, and therefore used in small quantities.

Roast barley (unmalted) is excellent in dry stouts, as is flaked barley. Other flaked grains—like breakfast cereals—are available. Flaked corn and flaked rice, for instance, are good in light dry beers and lagers, the corn flavor being useful in Carlsberg-type lagers and rice in American-style beers such as Coors and Budweiser, as can be seen from the formulation on the can of the latter. Wheat malt (grain, flake, or syrup) can be bought from specialist shops, and is essential for Weissen or Wheat beers. Rolled oats are rarely used now that oatmeal stout, like milk stout, has gone out of fashion. A point worth noting is that if you cannot buy these adjuncts from homebrew sources, some breakfast foods will do just as well—Shredded Wheat and Weetabix (wheat), cornflakes (corn), and Rice Krispies, for instance.

Another useful material is brewing flour, a wheat flour widely used in commercial breweries. In the mashing context, malt extract can also be regarded as an adjunct and used to reduce the cost.

As long as the proportion of adjuncts is kept low, they can be mashed with the bulk of the pale malt, but if larger quantities are used, they must be cooled separately first.

For instance, ½ lb. (225 g.) of crushed corn or ground rice and ¼ lb. (110 g.) malt can be heated in 2.5 quarts (2 liters) of water to 113°F (45°C) and held at this temperature for half an hour, then boiled for a quarter of an hour. This can then be mixed with a main mash, consisting say, of 1½ lb. (675 g.) malt, which has been steeped in 2.5 quarts (2 liters) of water at 100°F (38°C) and kept at 86°F (30°C) for another hour. Mashing then proceeds in the usual way.

The comparative starch contents, as percentages of dry substances, in a few common grits are: corn rice, 80-85; polished rice, 88-92; tapioca, 75-90; wheat, 65-78; potatoes, 65-75; oats, 60-70; rye, 60-65; and barley, 57-65. Some of these are often used to add body and strength to a thin beer. It is as well, however, to avoid this particular commercial practice, because risks of making poor beers that do not ferment or clear well are much increased.

Cracking

Before you can mash it, your malt must be cracked to render the starch freely available. It should be noted that cracked means what is says, i.e., crushed, rather than ground to a fine flour that will make clarification difficult. If the husks can be left whole, they later form a natural filter bed. So a device that will grind or crack only coarsely is required. I find a hand coffee mill of the old-fashioned type an ideal tool, the only trouble being that its hopper and receiving drawer are too small. A useful idea for a handyman is to remove the central grinding mechanism and build it into a larger hopper over a larger receptacle, such as a plastic bucket. The top part of a large polythene funnel makes an admirable hopper, or one can be constructed out of plywood.

An electric coffee mill is quite good, if adjustable, but otherwise tends to grind the malt too finely. One can also improvise by using a wooden rolling pin, or beer bottle as a roller, but this is apt to be rather a messy business, because grain tends to shoot everywhere, unless enclosed in a strong polythene or linen bag. A food processor is simple to use, but be careful not to reduce the grain to a powder.

A food processor can make the malt cracking process simple, as long as it is set to coarsely chop the malt rather than grind it.

Mashing

Crushed malt has then to be mashed to convert its starch to maltose, or sugar, and to extract it. Ideally, one needs a long mashing period, as much as eight hours, to obtain the fullest conversion and extraction, but many home brewers content themselves with a two-hour mashing, because it is in the first two hours that the major enzymatic activity occurs.

Mashing is the central and most important single process in brewing, and mash consistency and temperature control are vital if optimum conversion of starch and extraction are to be achieved.

The temperature of the mash should be between 145°F (62°C) and 155°F (68°C) and should never be allowed to rise above the latter figure. The best rule of thumb is to aim at an average of 150°F (65°C), within one or two degrees, and to go as high as 153°F (65°C) for light ales and bitter, or as low as 146°F

(63°C) for milds and browns. Temperature control is tricky, but can be achieved without too much difficulty, as will be seen.

If you are adopting the orthodox mashing and sparging method, on no account use more than 5 quarts (4.5 liters) of liquor to 1½ lb. (675 g.) malt for the two purposes combined, or you will extract more starch than you can convert and finish up with a beer that has a starch haze.

You will have worked out how much malt you need to use to produce the desired quantity of beer, but your initial mash needs to be a stiff one, with at least 4½ lb. of malt to 5 quarts of liquor (2 kg. to 4.5 liters).

Normally, if brewing a 20 or 25 quart batch (18-22.5 liters), it is necessary to use 10 quarts (9 liters) or so of water to mash the grain, and the remainder also hot, for sparging or rinsing it, so as to finish up with the correct quantity or length.

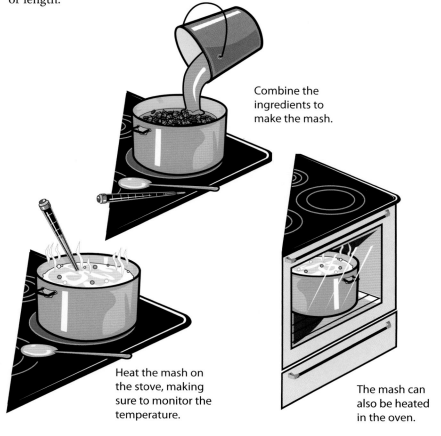

Combine the ingredients to make the mash.

Heat the mash on the stove, making sure to monitor the temperature.

The mash can also be heated in the oven.

There are three basic mashing methods you can use to successfully maintain the desired temperature accurately throughout the mashing process:

- A large saucepan or "dixie" (up to 15 quarts, 13.5 liters) on a source of heat or in an oven
- A 10-quart (9 liter) plastic bucket and an immersion heater
- A Bruheat or other electric boiler and a grain bag

In a saucepan

Usually you will be using pale malt, some cereal adjuncts, and perhaps some malt extract. If you are using a saucepan, they can all go in together.

You will need a really large saucepan—for years I used very successfully an old fashioned Army dixie—or a jam-making pan, and you need to allow a pint of water (500 ml.) for each pound (450 g.) of grain or diastatic malt extract. Heat the water to 131°F (55°C) and mix in the malt extract, followed by the grain malt and any adjuncts. Insert your thermometer and increase the heat to raise the temperature of the mash gradually to 155°F (68°C), stirring all the time to keep the mash from contact with the heated metal. Really thorough stirring is also always essential in any method of mashing, to prevent dry spots, which are surprisingly persistent.

Switch off the heat and the mash will (very slowly) begin to cool, so keep an eye on your thermometer. Remember that your aim is to maintain an average temperature of 150°F (65°C) for the next hour or so, so you can allow yourself to work in the range 145°F (62°C) to 155°F (68°C). When the temperature drops to 145°F (62°C), therefore, apply more heat, and stir again, to bring the temperature back to 155°F (68°C). You will probably need to do this only two or three times.

One way of maintaining temperature easily is to put your large saucepan, or Dixie, containing the hot mash in the gas oven (all shelves removed) on low, or in an electric oven set to maintain 145°-155°F (62°-68°C).

Iodine Test

After half an hour or so, test whether conversion is complete and you have reached starch end point. Drop a small sample of mash onto a white tile or plate and add to it a few drops of iodine. It should remain brown. If there is any trace of blue or blue-black, there is still some starch remaining and mashing must be continued. A second test can be made after a further quarter of an hour. When the sample remains brown, conversion is complete.

If all the starch has been successfully converted, the mash must then be strained into your boiler and sparged (rinsed) with the remaining water, also at 155°F (68°C), until you have the volume of beer you intended making. This you can do by scooping up the mash in a nylon flour sieve and rinsing it through with two or three pots full of hot water, as you would when cooking rice.

Not-Ready

Ready

In a bucket

You can mash in a 10-quart (9 liter) plastic bucket by employing a 50-watt immersion heater obtainable from homebrew firms. It is best to have as liquid a mash as possible in this case to avoid the grain being in contact with the heater. This means, again, constant agitation and care that the heater does not touch the side or bottom of the bucket.

If the results of your iodine test show there is still starch in the mash (if your mash sample turns blue instead of remaining brown), continue mashing and test again after fifteen minutes.

Some home brewers find close temperature control tedious, and adopt short cuts, which, while perhaps not producing immaculate results, are still satisfactory. The method is to infuse the malt in some of the liquor, and maintain an even temperature by means of a thermostat, making much longer mashing periods possible.

Here is an example: Use a 10-quart (9 liter) polythene bucket or boiler with lid. Bring just under 10 quarts (9 liters) of liquor to 150°F (65°C), pour in the bucket, and scatter in 2 lb. (1 kg.) of milled matt, or grist.

Then insert a 50-watt glass immersion heater, put the lid on the bucket, cover with a blanket or thick cloth, and leave on overnight or for a period of eight hours. The temperature with these quantities and with this type of heater will remain between 130°F (54°C) and 150°F (65°C) and extraction is first rate. Such a heater, costing little, will last for years and it is quite unnecessary even to have a thermostat. Alternatively, the mash will keep almost to temperature overnight in a picnic cooler, providing the box has been rinsed with hot water first and the liquor starts with a temperature of 165°F (74°C).

Strain off into a boiler and sparge to 15 or 20 quarts (13.5-18 liters). Add 2 oz. (55 g.) hops and 2 lb. (1 kg.) brewing (corn) sugar. Boil for an hour. Strain, cool to 75°F (24°C), ferment, prime, and bottle as usual.

A similar method, popular today, is to use large insulated water coolers for mashing. These containers help keep the mash at the proper temperature, and the spout allows the wort to be drawn off the grain easily.

Mashing in a bucket using an immersion heater will allow you to mash overnight.

Bruheat or Electric Boiler

You may, however, be lucky enough to have a boiler with a tap, and in this case, the job can be greatly simplified, particularly if it is a Bruheat, which is custom-built for the job. It is a large polypropylene bucket fitted with a tap, electric element, and thermostat, and is ideal for mashing, because it will hold the mash at a constant temperature. The Bruheat is light and easy to handle, and the electrical system dismantles easily and safely, so a thorough cleaning can be done after every use. It is therefore the best possible brewing tool. The Thorne Electrim and other electric boilers are very similar and work in the same way.

Use about 10 quarts (9 liters) of your total of 20 or 25 quarts (18-22.5 liters) for mashing. Pour it into the boiler and switch on. As it warms, pour in any malt extract you are using. Your pale grain malt and other grist, such as cereal flakes, are best contained in a grain bag of reasonably fine mesh and suspended in the boiler so that the grain is below the surface of the liquid, but clear of the element. Keep the top of the bag open so you can stir the mash with a large spoon or ladle.

Turn up the heat and keep stirring until you reach the magic mashing level of 150°F (65°C), then turn the dial of the thermostat slowly back until you can discover where it clicks on and off at that temperature. Leave it there. The Bruheat is then set, and will maintain the mash at that temperature indefinitely.

When conversion is shown to be complete by the iodine test, lift the grain bag clear of the wort and sparge with the remaining liquor, also at 150°F (65°C).

Bruheat bitter

As an example of the mashing and sparging technique, try Bruheat Bitter.

Using a Bruheat, a suitable recipe for 25 quarts (22.5 liters) of bitter is: 7 lb. (3 kg.) crushed pale malt, ½ lb. (225 g.) crushed crystal malt, 3 oz. (90 g.) Goldings hops, 2 lb. (1 kg.) brewing (corn) sugar (Itona), 1 teaspoon Leigh Williams pale ale water treatment (if you live in a soft water district), and dry beer finings.

Sparging

Whichever way you decide to mash, at the end of the process you will need to strain your wort into a boiler. Stretch a grain bag or nylon netting over the top of the boiler, secure it around the rim, and tip the mash into it. If, on the other hand, you have used a grain bag in the boiler, lift it clear of the wort and suspend it similarly.

Then "sparge," or rinse, the mash gently with the remainder of the liquor, which should be at a temperature of 170°F (75°C) or so at the outset to maintain that 150°F (65°C) mashing temperature. The wort running out should be at that temperature. If it is not, increase the temperature of the sparging liquor or turn up the heat. For sparging, use a very fine watering can or a hose set at a garden pressure spray, so you can do it gently (remember to make sure they are clean). This is rather a slow job, and to my mind the only tedious part of the mashed-beer process. I preheat the sparging liquor and then use it, 5 quarts (4.5 liters) at a time, from a watering can. This process is illustrated on the following three pages.

Brewing With an Electric Boiler

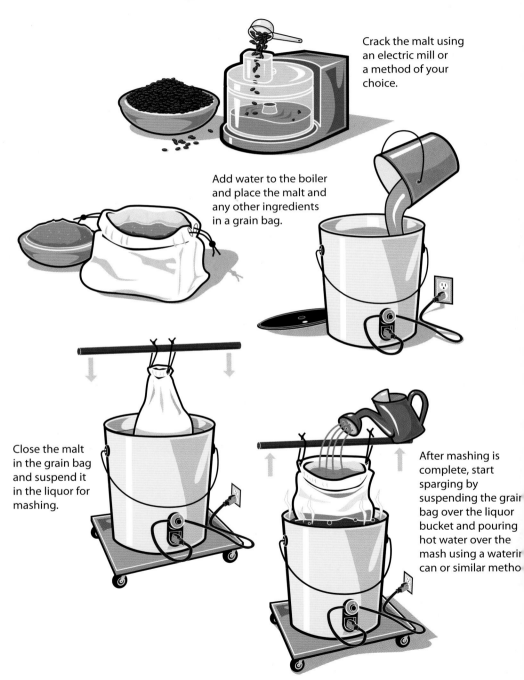

Crack the malt using an electric mill or a method of your choice.

Add water to the boiler and place the malt and any other ingredients in a grain bag.

Close the malt in the grain bag and suspend it in the liquor for mashing.

After mashing is complete, start sparging by suspending the grain bag over the liquor bucket and pouring hot water over the mash using a watering can or similar method.

Sparging can also be done by placing the mash in a sieve and pouring hot water over it.

Add brewing sugar to the wort produced after sparging.

Place hops in a nylon net bag with a long string and suspend the bag in the wort. The wort is now ready for boiling.

Boiling

Once sparging is complete, the wort must be thoroughly boiled to extract the flavor from the hops that are now added to it, to obtain the essential bitterness of beer. Any sugars used in the recipe can also be added at this stage. Use ½ oz. to 1½ oz. (15 g. to 45 g.) of hops per 5 quarts (4.5 liters), according to the degree of bitterness required, but hold back a small quantity to add in the last five minutes. (The aroma of the hops tends to be boiled out and this will restore it.) It is a good idea to enclose the hops loosely in a nylon net bag with a long string, for easy removal later. The wort must be boiled for at least thirty minutes, and preferably forty-five minutes. One point to note is that boiling does darken the beer. (Half an hour will give a pale beer, but less will give an anemic-looking one. Up to one and a half hours will produce a darker beer). For stouts and extra stouts, of course, black malt or roasted barley should be included. A good rolling boil is essential.

Fermenting

When the temperature has dropped to 60°F (15.5°C), strain off or remove the hops, give the wort a good rousing, and run it off into your fermenting bin. It pays to fit a scrap of nylon pot scourer in the inside end of the tap to prevent odd bits of grain or hops causing a blockage. Or protect the inlet with your long-handled spoon or a flour sieve. Pitch the yeast and ferment, rest, prime, and bottle as usual.

The Mashed Beer Process Summarized

1. Grind your malt and grits.

2. Bring 10 quarts (9 liters) or so of water to 155°F (68°C) and dissolve in it any diastatic malt extract.

3. Mash in your malt and grits, in a grain bag if necessary, at an average temperature of 150°F (65°C).

4. Test with iodine to ensure conversion is complete.

5. Strain into boiler and sparge with remaining water, at 150°F, 65°C (usually 10-15 quarts, 9-13.5 liters)

6. Add hops, any sugars, or plain malt extract.

7. Boil for at least an hour, adding a few hops in the last five minutes.

8. Cool, add yeast, and ferment as usual.

9. Rack, rest, and bottle.

True Beer Recipes

Lagers

Standard Lager
(20 quarts/18 liters)

Ingredients		
4 lb.	Pale malt (cracked)	2 kg.
2½ oz.	Hallertauer hops	70 g.
3 lb.	Sugar	1.3 kg.
	Lager yeast	
½ heaping teaspoon	Citric acid	
20 quarts	Water (soft)	18 liters

Method:

Mash as described, using 10 quarts (9 liters) of water, in a Bruheat, with the malt in a suspended brew bag. Then strain the wort into the boiler, add 2 oz. (55 g.) hops, salt, and the remaining water. Bring to the boil and simmer for forty minutes. Add a few loose hops (½ oz., 15 g. or so). Simmer for five minutes.

Put the sugar and the citric acid into a 25-quart (22.5 liter) polythene brewbin and strain the wort onto them. Add the balance of the water, cold, and stir thoroughly until all sugar is dissolved. Cool to 75°F (24°C), then add lager yeast and nutrient.

Lager yeast is a bottom fermenter—it eventually settles well. The first head of froth that forms on the brew after two days should be skimmed off. Fermentation will normally take a week in a warm place. Keep the container well covered. Bottle when SG is about 1005 and certainly not above 1010, or when surface of brew clears, but tiny bubbles are visible in a ring in the middle. Add half a level teaspoon sugar to each pint of beer (500 ml.), fill to within ½ in. (about 1 cm.) of stopper, and seal. Store upright in cool place for at least a month.

Pilsner-Type Lager

(This recipe by Dave Line makes 10 quarts (9 liters) of Pilsner-type lager
(OG 1032) and 10 quarts of strong lager simultaneously. Brew 20 quarts
(18 liters) of the low gravity lager, keep ten as Pilsner, and add golden syrup
to ferment the remainder to a strong brew.)

Ingredients		
4 lb.	Crushed lager malt	2 kg.
1 lb.	Flaked corn	450 g.
2 lb.	Golden syrup	1 kg.
2½ oz.	Hallertauer hops	70 g.
	Lager yeast	
20 quarts	Soft water (remove chalk by pre-boiling if necessary)	18 liters

Method:

Heat 15 quarts (13.5 liters) of water up to 125°-130°F (51°-54°C) and stir in the crushed lager malt and flaked corn. Leave to stand for half an hour.

Stirring continuously, slowly raise the temperature of the mash up and leave it again, ensuring the mash stays as near to, but not exceeding, 150°F (65°C) for another half an hour or so until starch end point is passed.

Strain off from the grain (best held in a large grain bag) and sparge (rinse) with hot water around 160°F (71°C) to collect 20 quarts (18 liters) of liquid.

Boil the wort with 1½ oz. (45 g.) of the hops for an hour and a half. Switch off and stir in the rest of the hops. Stir the hops in the wort two or three more times over the next quarter of an hour.

Strain off into a fermenting bin, taking care to leave the hops and protein debris behind. Top up with cold water to the 20-quart (18 liter) mark.

When cool to 60°F (15°C), pitch a working lager yeast starter. Try to maintain the temperature below 65°F (17°C) to avoid off flavors from the bottom-fermenting yeast. Skim off any dirty yeast that forms.

After four to five days when the SG falls to around 1007, rack off into a clean container and add gelatin finings.

Two days later, prepare four 5-quart (4.5 liter) jars. To two of them add 1 lb. (450 g.) of golden syrup dissolved in the same volume of warm water (1 lb. for each bottle).

Siphon the clear beer into the 5-quart (4.5 liter) jars and fit airlocks.

The two jars without the syrup contain the Pilsner lager, which can be bottled after another week's rest. Besides priming each bottle with sugar, Krausen with a few grains of lager yeast. Mature for one month in the bottle before drinking.

The special brew lager will ferment for another week using up the golden syrup. When fermentation abates, rack off into other 5-quart (4.5 liter) jars and let it rest for two weeks before bottling.

This time, dip the siphon tube momentarily into the yeast sediment to carry over sufficient cells to act on the priming sugar. This one is worth maturing for at least two months in the bottle before drinking.

Ales

London Light Ale

(25 quarts/22.5 liters)

Ingredients		
4 lb.	Crushed pale malt	1.8 kg.
½ lb.	Flaked rice	230 g.
1 lb.	Brewing (corn) sugar	450 g.
2 oz.	Goldings hops	55 g.
	Beer yeast	
25 quarts	Water	22.5 liters.

Method:

Collect 10 quarts (9 liters) of water from hot tap and add ½ heaping teaspoon of lactic acid water treatment. Mix in the ground pale malt and flaked rice. Mash as directed and sparge to collect 15 quarts (13.5 liters) of wort. Boil the wort with the hops for one hour before straining off into the fermentation bin. Stir in the brewing (corn) sugar until dissolved. Top up to 25 quarts (22.5 liters) with cold water. When cool, add the yeast and ferment until the SG falls to 1007 before racking off into a fresh container to rest.

Classic Pale Ale

(25 quarts/22.5 liters), Original Gravity 1045

Ingredients		
5 lb.	Crushed pale malt	2.25 kg.
2 lb.	Diastatic malt extract	1 kg.
4 oz.	Brewing flour	100 g.
2 oz.	Fuggles hops	55 g.
3 oz.	Goldings hops	90 g.
1 lb.	Brewing (corn) sugar	450 g.
25 quarts	Water	22.5 liters
	Water treatment for Pale Ale	
	Irish moss	
	Commercial brewing yeast (if possible)	

Method:

Add the water treatment to 15 quarts (13.5 liters) of water and raise the temperature to 150°F (65°C). Dissolve the malt extract in the hot water. Dry mix the brewing flour and the cracked pale malt and then slowly stir this in as well. Continue stirring while raising the temperature slowly (say over five minutes) back to 150°F (65°C). Mash for two hours. Sparge (rinse) the grains with hot water to collect 22.5 quarts (20 liters) of wort.

Measure out 1 oz. (30 g.) of the Goldings hops and add these with the Fuggles to the wort and boil for at least one hour. Use the Irish moss as directed in the instructions. Switch off the boiler and allow the solids to settle. Hold the remaining 2 oz. (55 g.) of Goldings in a large grain bag or strainer below the boiler tap. Position a collection vessel below the strainer. Crack open the boiler tap and let the hot wort percolate gently through the hops to extract some of their finer flavoring properties.

Dissolve the brewing (corn) sugar in a few pints (500 ml. or more) of hot water and add this to the fermenting bin as well. Top up the wort to 25 quarts (22.5 liters) with pre-boiled water. When the wort cools to 70°F (20°C), stir in a yeast starter cultivated from a commercial yeast.

Ferment four to five days until the SG falls to 1012 and then rack off into a 25-quart (22.5 liter) fresh container to rest. Add ½ oz. (15 g.) of gelatin in solution for fining. Bottle four days later in primed beer bottles.

Economy Pale Ale
(12.5 quarts/11 liters)

Ingredients		
½ lb.	Crushed corn or ground rice	225 g.
1¾ lb.	Malt	900 g.
12.5 quarts	Water	11 liters
	Yeast	
1¾ oz.	Goldings hops	50 g.

Method:

Make your main mash by steeping 1½ lb. (675 g.) cracked malt in 2.5 quarts (2 liters) of water at 101°F (38°C) for a quarter of an hour. Keep at 86°F (30°C) for a further hour. Meanwhile, crack ½-1 lb. (225-450 g.) of corn (or rice) and ¼ lb. (110 g.) malt with a rolling pin or mincer, put into 2.5 quarts (2 liters) of water, and bring up to 113°F (45°C). Hold at this temperature for half an hour, then boil for a further quarter of an hour. Mix your two mashes. Raise the temperature to 160°F (72°C) for the starch to sugar conversion to proceed. When this is complete, as shown by an iodine test, heat the brew to 167°F (75°C) to stabilize it. The solids should then be allowed to settle and the clear wort is then run off and made up to 12.5 quarts (11 liters) with more water. Add 2 oz. (55 g.) hops and a heaping teaspoon of salt. Bring to the boil, and simmer for two hours. Cool to 70°F (20°C), pitch the yeast, ferment, and bottle as usual.

Strong Pale Ale

(20 quarts/18 liters)

Ingredients		
6 lb.	Malt	3 kg.
4 lb.	Sugar	2 kg.
4 oz.	Goldings hops	100 g.
20 quarts	Water (hard)	18 liters
	Brewer's yeast	

Method:

Crack the malt.

Measure out 20 quarts (18 liters) of water and bring 10 quarts (9 liters) of it to 150°F (65°C). Put the malt into a 10-quart (9 liter) polythene bucket and pour onto it as much water as possible. Insert 50-watt immersion heater, cover and wrap bucket with blanket, and switch on. Leave heater on for eight hours, keeping the temperature of the liquor at about 150°F (65°C). Then strain the wort into a boiler. Add 3 oz. (90 g.) hops and salt. Bring to the boil and simmer for forty minutes. Add another 1 oz. (30 g.) hops and simmer for further five minutes.

Put the sugar into a polythene brewbin and strain the wort onto it through a nylon sieve. Stir well, bring the quantity up to 20 quarts (18 liters) with cold water, and stir thoroughly to make sure all sugar is dissolved. Allow to cool to 70°F (21°C), then cream your yeast in a pudding basin half filled with the wort. Pour this barm back into the brew. Ferment and continue as usual, priming and bottling after nine or ten days.

Birmingham Ale

(20 quarts/18 liters)

Ingredients		
4 lb.	Pale malt (crushed)	2 kg.
3 oz.	Goldings hops	90 g.
20 quarts	Water	18 liters
2 lb.	Crystal malt (cracked)	1 kg.
1½ lb.	Brewing (corn) sugar	700 g.
	Brewer's yeast	

Method:

Bring about 6 pints (3 liters) water to 170°F (77°C) and pour into warmed enamel bucket. Add the grain and test temperature. If this has dropped below 150°F (65°C), raise to this figure with hot water until temperature is uniform throughout the mash. Place in gas oven (all shelves removed) on low (verity that this is the correct setting for your oven) and leave to mash for two hours.

Now strain into boiler. Add water to 20 quarts (18 liters) and the brewing (corn) sugar and the hops, but keep back about ½ oz. (15 g.) of the latter until later. Boil for two hours then add the ½ oz. (15 g.) of hops and simmer for five minutes.

Strain into fermenting bin and leave to cool to 70°F (21°C)

Take SG. This should be about 1040-1045, which will give a potential alcoholic content of 4.5%. Pitch yeast and ferment down to 1010 before barreling (about three days). Prime with 16 teaspoons of castor sugar and add about one-third of a pint (150 ml.) of Leigh-Williams Beer Finings.

'Amber Glow' Stock Ale

(15 quarts/13.5 liters), Original Gravity 1066

Ingredients		
4 lb.	Crushed pale malt	2 kg.
1 lb.	Crushed amber malt	450 g.
2 lb.	Natural brown sugar*	1 kg.
4 oz.	Fuggles hops	125 g.
3 teaspoons	Brewer's yeast	15 ml.
½ teaspoon/pint	White sugar to condition	5 mg./liter
15 quarts	Water	13.5 liters

Method:

Use permanently hard water, mashing in 12.5 quarts (11 liters) and collecting, after sparging, 15 quarts (13.5 liters) of liquid. Boil with the hops for an hour and a half and strain off into a fermenting vessel. Add natural brown sugar dissolved as a syrup. When cool, pitch in the yeast and ferment and bottle as usual.

Natural brown sugar is made through the partial refinement of sugar cane extract. Adding molasses to fully refined sugar is how most brown sugar is made. Natural brown sugar is generally drier and paler, and has larger crystals than standard brown sugar.

Mild Ale

(20 quarts/18 liters)

Ingredients		
4 lb.	Crystal malt (cracked)	2 kg.
1 lb.	Flaked corn	450 g.
4 lb.	Dark brown sugar	2 kg.
20 quarts	Water (soft)	18 liters
1 tablespoon	Caramel	
4 oz.	Fuggles hops	100 g.
	Yeast and nutrient	
1 teaspoon	Each salt and citric acid	

Method:

The ale is best made by those living in a soft water district.

Crack the malt. Bring 10 quarts (9 liters) of water to 150°F (65°C). Put the malt and flaked corn into 10-quart (9 liter) polythene bucket and pour onto it as much water as possible. Insert 50-watt immersion heater and mash for eight hours at 150°F (65°C). Then strain the wort into a boiler, add 3½ oz. (90 g.) hops, and the salt. Bring to the boil and simmer for forty minutes. Add another ½ oz. (15 g.) hops and the
caramel (gravy browning liquid) and simmer for further five minutes.

Put the sugar into a polythene fermenter with the citric acid, and strain the wort onto it through a nylon sieve. Bring the quantity up to 20 quarts (18 liters) with cold water and stir thoroughly to make sure all sugar is dissolved. Allow to cool to 70°F (21°C), then cream your yeast in a pudding basin half filled with the wort, and pour this barm back into the brew. Cover closely and leave in a warm place for eight to ten days. Ferment out, rest, prime, and bottle as usual.

Brown Ale (1)

(20 quarts/18 liters)

Ingredients		
8 oz.	Crystal malt (cracked)	225 g.
1 lb.	Black malt (lightly cracked)	450 g.
3 oz.	Fuggles hops	85 g.
20 quarts	Water (soft)	18 liters
1 lb.	Brewing flour	450 g.
4 lb.	DMS malt extract	2 kg.
	Munton's beer yeast	
1 lb.	Brewing (corn) sugar	450 g.

Method:

Follow normal mashing procedure. If you wish to increase the body add, say, 8 oz. (225 g.) flaked barley.

Brown Ale (2)

(20 quarts/18 liters)

Ingredients		
5 lb.	Pale malt	2.25 kg.
4 lb.	Roasted malt	2 kg.
2 lb.	Brewing (corn) sugar	1 kg.
2 teaspoons	Salt	
2½ oz.	Fuggles hops	70 g.
20 quarts	Water (softened, if necessary)	18 liters
	Brewer's yeast	

Method:

Measure out your 20 quarts of water and bring up to 150°F (65°C) in a Bruheat or other electric boiler. Put the malt into a brew bag and infuse in the water. Leave heater on for two hours, keeping temperature between 145°F (62°C) and 155°F (68°C). Then lift out and drain the bag, add the hops and salt, bring to the boil, and simmer for forty minutes. Add ½ oz. (15 g.) loose hops and simmer for further five minutes. Put the brewing (corn) sugar into a 25-quart (22.5 liter) polythene fermenter, and strain the wort onto it through a nylon sieve. Stir well to amalgamate, then stir thoroughly again. Cool to 70°F (20°C) before adding the yeast. Ferment and continue as usual.

Best Brown Ale

(25 quarts/22.5 liters)

Ingredients		
5 lb.	Crushed pale ale or mild ale malt	2.25 kg.
½ lb.	Crushed wheat malt	225 g.
3½ oz.	Crushed black malt	110 g.
½ lb.	Natural brown sugar	225 g.
1 lb.	Brewing (corn) sugar	450 g.
2½ oz.	Hallertauer hops	75 g.
1	Sachet of dried beer yeast	
	Sweetex liquid	
	Heading liquid	
25 quarts	Water	22.5 liters

Method:

Mash the crushed malt in soft water between 145°-155°F (63°-68°C) for an hour and a half. Strain and sparge to collect 20 quarts (18 liters) of liquor. Boil with the hops for one hour and strain into a fermenting bin. Top up with the sugar quota in solution and cold water to the final quantity. When cool, add the yeast and ferment four to six days until the SG falls to 1008. Rack off and keep under airlock protection for a few days before bottling. Add to each bottle ½ teaspoon of white sugar, one drop of heading liquid, and one drop of Sweetex liquid per pint (500 ml.) of capacity. Mature for two weeks before sampling.

Bitters

Traditional Bitter

(20 quarts/18 liters), Original Gravity 1045

Ingredients		
7 lb.	Crushed pale malt	3.5 kg.
4 oz.	Hallertauer hops	125 g.
2 oz.	Brown sugar	55 g.
	Beer yeast	
	Beer finings	
20 quarts	Water	18 liters

Method:

Mix the crushed malt with hot tap water to form a smooth porridge. Raise the temperature to 155°F (68° C) and mash for another hour. Strain off the hot wort and rinse the grains gently to bring up to 20 quarts (18 liters) of liquid. Add the hops and boil for an hour and a half. Carefully strain off the clear wort from the hops and protein debris. Top up to the final quantity with cold water.

Ferment and finish as usual.

Crystal Crown Bitter

(25 quarts/22.5 liters)

Crystal Crown is an excellent best draught bitter brewed with the minimum of fuss and time. Although it is a grain beer using mashing techniques, it can be brewed in an evening quite easily.

Ingredients		
7 lb.	Crushed pale malt	3.5 kg.
5 oz.	Crushed crystal malt	150 g.
4 oz.	Brewing flour	100 g.
2 oz.	Bramling Cross or Fuggles hops	55 g.
3 oz.	Best Goldings hops	85 g.
2 oz.	Golden syrup	1 kg.
4 tablespoons	Sticky molasses	
	Brewer's yeast starter	
	Irish moss	
	Lactic acid water treatment	
25 quarts	Water	22.5 liters

Method:

Some brewing flour is included to increase the head retention of the beer. Where chalky waters are encountered, a teaspoon of lactic acid can speed up the reactions. This is added to 15 quarts (13.5 liters) of water in the Bruheat of other electric boiler after the temperature has reached 150°F (65°C). Slowly stir in the grains premixed with the flour, ensuring that there are no dry spots. Increase the heat setting and stir the goods continuously until the temperature reaches 150°F (65°C) again. Taking this extra care at the start of mashing should ensure that the starch end point is passed within half an hour so long as the temperature is maintained at 144°-150°F (62°-65°C).

Transfer the goods after one hour's mashing to the grain bag and sparge with hot water to collect 22.5 quarts (20 liters) of wort. Return the wort to the boiler and boil vigorously for forty-five minutes without the hops. Use the Irish moss in the boil as directed on the instructions. Switch off the boiler and stir in hops. Give the hops two or three more stirs at five minute intervals before allowing them to settle.

Please restrain your natural brewing instinct and don't be tempted to boil the hops.

Strain off the wort and add the golden syrup and molasses dissolved first in a few pints (500 ml. or more) of hot water. Top up to 25 quarts (22.5 liters) with cold water.

When cool, add the yeast and ferment, rack, rest, prime, and barrel as usual.

Whitbread Trophy-Style Bitter

(25 quarts/22.5 liters). Original Gravity 1037

Ingredients		
4 lb.	Crushed pale malt	2 kg.
5 oz.	Torrified barley	150 g.
12.5 quarts	Water for "bitter" brewing	11 liters
1 teaspoon	Irish moss	5 g.
1 lb.	Barley syrup or brewing (corn) sugar	450 g.
1 lb.	Soft dark brown sugar	450 g.
2 oz.	Fuggles hops	60 g.
(1 + ¼ + ¼) oz.	Goldings hops	(30 + 10 + 10) g.
2 oz.	Brewer's yeast	60 g.
	Whitbread Trophy if possible	
½ oz.	Gelatin	15 g.
2 oz.	Brown sugar	60 g.
25 quarts	Water	22.5 liters

Method:

Mash as usual and rinse the grains to collect 20 quarts (18 liters) of extract.

Boil the extract with the Fuggles hops and the first quota of Goldings hops for an hour and a half. Dissolve the main batch of sugar and barley syrup or brewing (corn) sugar in a little hot water, and add this and the second batch of Goldings during the boil. Also pitch in the Irish moss as directed on the instructions.

Switch off the heat, stir in the third batch of Goldings, and allow them to soak for fifteen minutes. Strain off the clear wort into a fermenting bin and top up the final quantity with cold water.

Ferment, rack, rest, and put into primed pressure barrel as usual.

Bridgend Bitter

(25 quarts/22.5 liters), Original Gravity 1050

Ingredients		
7 lb.	Crushed pale malt	3.5 kg.
12 oz.	Crushed crystal malt	340 g.
4 oz.	Flaked barley	100 g.
1 oz.	Crushed black malt	30 g.
1 lb.	Golden syrup	450 g.
1 teaspoon	Irish moss	5 g.
2 oz.	Sugar for priming	60 g.
	Brewer's yeast starter	
3 oz.	East Kent Golding hops	90 g.
2 oz.	Fuggles hops	60 g.
1 packet	Davis' gelatin	
25 quarts	Water	22.5 liters

Method:

Mash the grain with 15 quarts (13.5 liters) of water for two hours to ensure a higher proportion of dextrinous sugars.

Sparge to collect 25 quarts (22.5 liters).

Boil with the hops and the golden syrup for two hours adding Irish moss halfway through the boil.

Strain off the wort and cool rapidly to achieve the cold break. Top up with cold water to 25 quarts (22.5 liters).

Pitch the yeast and stir vigorously to aerate the wort.

Thereafter continue as usual, fining with gelatin before putting beer into primed barrel.

Bitter

(20 quarts/18 liters)

Ingredients		
2 lb.	Crystal malt	1 kg.
2 lb.	Tin golden syrup	1 kg.
	Beer yeast	
2 lb.	Pale malt	1 kg.
3 oz.	Golding hops	85 g.
20 quarts	Water (hard)	18 liters

Method:

Mash the malts in the boiler at 150°F (65°C) for four hours. Strain off. Add the hops and some salt and boil for an hour. Strain again and add the syrup. Allow to cool to below 75°F (24°C) and add the yeast. Ferment at between 63°-68°F (17°-20°C) for four days. Then prime and barrel as usual.

Barley Wine (1)

(5 quarts/4.5 liters)

by P. Bryant

True barley wine can only be made successfully by using good quality pale malted barley as the main ingredient. Malt extract will never give the full malty flavor required, whatever quantity is used.

The best adjunct to use is flaked rice or polished barley, which help to provide body. You can try flaked corn, cornflakes, ground rice, oat flakes, and dried bananas, but for this recipe one of the two above-mentioned adjuncts is to be preferred.

Ingredients		
1¾ lb.	Pale malted barley	800 g.
2 oz.	Flaked rice or 4 oz. (100 g.) polished barley	55 g.
1 oz.	Fuggles hops	30 g.
1 lb.	Sugar	450 g.
1 teaspoon	Citric acid	
5 quarts	Water	4.5 liters
1 teaspoon	Ammonium sulfate	
1 teaspoon	Gypsum	
½ teaspoon	Salt	
1	Campden tablet	
	Champagne yeast	

Method:

Pick over and then put malted barley and adjunct through mincer to form the grist.

Heat 5 quarts (4.5 liters) of water to 154°F (68°C) in 12-pint (5.5 liter) saucepan on very low gas. Add grist and mash for two hours.

Strain through kitchen sieve and then replace wort in saucepan. Add hops and gypsum and boil for forty minutes. Strain again, cool, and take SG, which should be around 1048.

Add sugar, Campden tablet, citric acid, ammonium sulfate, salt, and champagne yeast and commence fermenting in a 10-quart (4.5 liters) polythene bucket with lid. Fermentation will be strong within twelve hours. Skim brown scum from surface each day and after two days, siphon into 5-quart (4.5 liter) jar and fit fermentation lock. When clearing begins (which may be after six weeks), rack and refit lock. When clear, rack again, cork, and store for six months, after which it may be bottled.

Barley Wine (2)

(15 quarts/13.5 liters)

by Wilf Newsom

Ingredients		
5 lb.	Pale malt	2.25 kg.
1 oz.	Black malt	30 g.
3 teaspoons	Gypsum	
	Natural sugar to gravity 1083 (approx. 1 lb., 450 g.)	
	Beer and champagne yeast blended, and later a general purpose wine yeast	
1 lb.	Crystal malt	450 g.
4 oz.	Wheat syrup	120 g.
3½ oz.	Whitbread Golding hops	110 g.
15 quarts	Water	13.5 liters

Method:

Bring water to 154°F (65°C). Add grist (crushed grains) and mash for two hours at 144°-154°F (62°-68°C), or to starch end point (clear wort). Strain off, add gypsum and hops and boil for forty minutes. Strain off. Gravity should be approximately 1048. Add sugar as syrup to a gravity of 1083. When cool, add blend of active beer and champagne yeast. After skimming, transfer into 5-quart (4.5 liter) jars, fit airlocks, and allow fermentation to proceed. When the gravity has reached the 1020 mark, the fermentation will show signs of stopping. At this stage, pitch in activated general purpose wine yeast and ferment out. Bottle and prime in nips of 6½ fl. oz. (180 ml.) or ½ pint (250 ml.) Keep for at least twelve months before serving.

Jubilee Ale—Bitter

(10 quarts/9 liters), Original Gravity 1095

by Dave Line

A good permanently hard water is essential for mashing this grist. Add 1 teaspoon of gypsum to 15 quarts (13.5 liters) of mashing liquor.

Ingredients		
6 lb.	Crushed pale malt	3 kg.
2 lb.	Crushed lager malt	1 kg.
1 lb.	Soft brown sugar	450 g.
3 oz.	East Kent Goldings hops	90 g.
1 oz.	Styrian Goldings or Bramling Cross hops	30 g.
	Good quality general purpose yeast	

Method:

Mash by the standard method and sparge to collect just over 15 quarts (13.5 liters) of wort.

Add the hops and sugar and boil the mix for at least an hour or until the volume has been reduced to 12.5 quarts (11 liters). Let the wort settle for fifteen minutes after the boil before carefully straining off the clear wort from the bed of hops into another container fitted with an airlock.

When cool, the wort should have a gravity of between 1090 and 1100 to give the brew the alcohol potential of a table wine. Pitch in the wine yeast and ferment for a week or so until the vigorous activity abates. Complete the fermentation in two 5-quart (4.5 liter) jars. Just like normal wine procedures, rack the brew off the heavy sediment into fresh jars. Here the ale will eventually fall bright, leaving a thin deposit of yeast on the bottom.

Add 2 teaspoons of white sugar dissolved in a little warm water to each of two fresh 5-quart (4.5 liter) jars. Rack the clear beer into them, ensuring a little yeast is carried over. Fit airlocks and wait for the fermentation to restart before bottling in nip or half-pint bottles (250 ml.).

Stouts

Andover Stout

(20 quarts/18 liters)

Ingredients		
4 lb.	Pale malt (crushed)	2 kg.
2 lb.	Black malt	1 kg.
2 lb.	Crystal malt (crushed)	1 kg.
2 lb.	Brewing (corn) sugar or golden syrup	1 kg.
2½ oz.	Fuggles hops	75 g.
2 teaspoons	Salt	
½ teaspoon	Citric acid	
	Brewer's yeast	
20 quarts	Water (softened)	18 liters

Method:

Mash the three malts in a brew bag in 10 quarts (9 liters) of water in a Bruheat or other electric boiler.

Start with the water at 150°F (65°C) and set the boiler to hold the temperature at 145°F-155°F (62°C-68°C) for two hours. Then remove the bag and let it drain. Make up to 20 quarts (18 liters), add 2 oz. (55 g.) hops and salt, and bring to the boil. Boil for forty minutes, add the remaining hops, and boil for a further five. Put the golden syrup and citric acid into your brew bin and strain the wort onto them. Stir thoroughly. When cool, add the yeast starter and continue as usual.

Birmingham Stout

(20 quarts/18 liters)

Ingredients		
4 lb.	Pale malt (crushed)	2 kg.
1 lb.	Roasted (or black) malt	450 g.
1½ lb.	Brewing (corn) sugar	675 g.
3 oz.	Hops	85 g.
	Brewer's yeast	
1 lb.	Crystal malt	450 g.
1 lb.	Flaked barley	450 g.
1 teaspoon	Salt	
20 quarts	Water	18 liters

Method:

As for Birmingham Ale (page 107).

Milk Stout

(20 quarts/18 liters)

Ingredients		
2 lb.	Patent black malt	1 kg.
6 oz.	Flaked barley	170 g.
2 lb.	Glucose (powdered)	1 kg.
20 quarts	Water (soft)	18 liters
4 lb.	Pale malt (crushed)	2 kg.
	Brewer's yeast	
2 oz.	Hops	55 g.
1 teaspoon	Salt	

Method:

Culture a good quality beer yeast.

Bring 20 quarts of water up to 150°F (65°C) in a boiler and mash the malts and barley as described. (The black malt gives your stout the desired dark coloring and woody tang, while the barley, or grit, provides extra strength economically.) Then strain the wort back into the boiler, add 1½ oz. (45 g.) of hops and the salt, bring to the boil, and simmer for forty minutes. Add the remaining ½ oz. (15 g.) of hops and simmer for five minutes. Put the 2 lb. (1 kg.) powdered glucose or brewing (corn) sugar into a brew bin and strain the wort onto them. Stir thoroughly. Bring the total volume up to 20 quarts (18 liters) by adding the remainder of the water, cold, and stir again.

When cool, add the yeast starter and stand container, closely covered, in a warm place. The fermentation will be going well after forty-eight hours. Skim on the third day. Ferment, rest, prime, and bottle as usual.

Sweet Stout

(25 quarts/22.5 liters)

Ingredients		
3½ lb.	Pale malt	1.6 kg.
6 oz.	Crystal malt	180 g.
3½ oz.	Whitbread Golding hops	115 g.
	Beer yeast	
½ lb.	Caramel (or 4 teaspoons of gravy browning liquid)	230 g.
8 oz.	Porage oats	240 g.
	Sweetex (liquid)	
	Natural brown sugar to gravity 1035	

Method:

Crush malts, add oats, and mash at 138°F (58°C). When starch free, run off wort and boil with hops and caramel for thirty-five minutes. Add sugar as syrup until SG 1035 is reached. Chill rapidly, add active yeast, and ferment out at 60°F (15°C). Just before bottling, taste beer. Add Sweetex to taste (four drops equals 1 teaspoon of sugar). As this is an unfermentable sweetening agent, there is no danger of further fermentation. Bottle and prime in the normal way. Keep for four weeks before serving.

Irish-Type Stout

(25 quarts/22.5 liters)

Ingredients		
7 lb.	Pale malt	3.5 kg.
4 oz.	Hops	110 g.
3 lb.	Natural brown sugar (as syrup)	1.3 kg.
½ lb.	Brown malt	250 g.
12½ oz.	Crystal malt	375 g.
2 oz.	Black malt	55 g.
3 oz.	Chocolate malt	90 g.
	Beer yeast	
25 quarts	Water	22.5 liters

Method:

Crush and mash all the grains at a temperature of 146°F (63°C) for an hour, then drop to 138°-140°F (57°-60°C) until mash runs clear. Strain off, add syrup and hops, and boil gently for thirty minutes. When temperature drops to 60°F (15°C), add activated yeast and ferment out. Bottle and keep for at least eight weeks before opening.

Oatmeal Stout

(20 quarts/18 liters)

Ingredients		
¾ lb.	Rye	350 g.
½ lb.	Black malt	225 g.
1½ lb.	Pale malt	675 g.
2 teaspoons	Brewer's yeast and nutrient	
6 oz.	Oatmeal	180 g.
2 oz.	Fuggles hops	55 g.
3 lb.	Sugar	1.3 kg.
½ teaspoon	Citric acid	
20 quarts	Water (soft)	18 liters

Method:

Bring 10 quarts of water up to 150°F (65°C) in a boiler. Pour most of this into a polythene 10-quart bucket, and then sprinkle in the malts, rye, and oatmeal. Insert a 50-watt immersion heater and switch on. Cover bucket closely with blanket and wrap it to conserve heat. Keep the heater on for eight hours, holding the temperature between 145°F and 155°F (62°C and 68°C). Then strain the wort back into the boiler, add 1½ oz. (45 g.) of hops and some salt, bring to the boil, and simmer for forty minutes. Add the remaining ½ oz. (15 g.) of hops and simmer for five minutes. Put the 4 lb. (2 kg.) sugar and the citric acid into a brewbin and strain the wort onto them. Stir thoroughly, bring the total volume up to 20 quarts (18 liters) by adding the remainder of the water, cold, and stir again.

Ferment and continue as usual.

CHAPTER 12

MALT EXTRACT BEERS

Malt extract beers may be made from a range of extracts, which are not necessarily hopped, as are those in most kits, thus giving the brewer greater economy and the chance of selecting his or her own hops and adjuncts.

The extract is dissolved in hot water and boiled with the hops and any malt or grits included in order to improve or change the flavor. Any remaining water can be added cold.

Extract beers are more economical, of course, and the whole range of beers and stouts is still within your grasp. The big advantages are that they are inexpensive to make and you avoid the mashing and sparging necessary when brewing from grain malt. There is a slight sacrifice of quality, however, compared with mashed beers, in most home brewers' opinions.

Malt extract varies greatly in quality and specification, so it pays to be careful what you buy. Chemists sell ordinary (unhopped) malt extract usually in 1 lb. or 2 lb. (½ kg. or 1 kg.) glass jars. Avoid that flavored with cod liver oil for obvious reasons. The best brewing extract, however, is usually sold in 2 lb. or 4 lb. (1 kg. or 2 kg.) tins. It is naturally cheaper if purchased in bulk, in 7 lb. or 14 lb. (3.5 kg. or 6 kg.) plastic tubs, or in even bigger quantities.

It is a good policy to buy a diastatic extract, i.e., one that has the power of converting the starch in any other grain used in the brew to fermentable sugar.

Check whether it is already hopped. Unhopped extract is usually cheaper.

The best brewing grades have the right balance for the production of body and alcohol, the right protein balance for good clearing and head retention, freedom from bacterial infection that could cause off flavors, and a standardized low color, so that you can tint up to your own requirements with roasted malts or caramel.

The big disadvantage of beers made entirely from extract is that they sometimes have a characteristic nutty flavor that is quite distinctive. Some do not find it disagreeable, but if you do, it can be minimized by using, say, 1 lb. of crystal malt or 1 lb. of roasted barley. This should be cracked with a mincer and boiled with the hops. Or you can use 1 lb. (450 g.) of unmalted whole barley in each 20 or 25 quarts (18-22.5 liters). Soak the barley in water for two or three days, pressure cook for thirty minutes in 3 pints (1.5 liters) of water (or boil until grains split), and then boil this barley mash with the hops and extract.

If one wishes to economize, household sugar can be substituted for some of the malt, and one can thus obtain varying strengths of flavor and varying alcoholic strengths. A good rule of thumb is that 1½-2 lb. (500 g.-1 kg.) of sugar (i.e., the combined weight of extract and sugar) per 5 quarts (4.5 liters) will give an exceedingly strong beer, and below 1 lb. (450 g.) per 5 quarts (4.5 liters) will produce weaker beers.

So all you need to remember is that the total sugar can range anywhere between 1 lb. and 2 lb. (450 g.-1 kg.) per 5 quarts (4.5 liters), counting extract and household sugar pound for pound. But do not fall into the trap, for reasons of false economy, of using a high proportion of sucrose, or the quality of the beer will suffer.

From the following table, which was devised by expert home brewer the late Humfrey Wakefield some years ago and since then has been used successfully by thousands of brewers all over the world, you can compile your own recipes to obtain exactly the brew you require.

Those who want a light beer for summer drinking in quantity will prefer No. 1, those who want an ordinary bitter strength will choose No. 2, those who want best bitter strength, No. 3, and those who want really strong beer of barley wine strength, No. 4. The stronger the beer, the less it can be drunk in quantity and, of course, the more expensive it is to make. Most home brewers will come to prefer the strength of No. 2 and 3.

To make 25 Quarts (22.5 liters)				
Recipe	1	2	3	4
Alcohol	3%	5%	7%	9%
Gravity at start	1030	1045	1060	1080
Gravity at finish	998	1000	1005	1009
Quarts water	25 (22.5 liters)	25 (22.5 liters)	25 (22.5 liters)	25 (22.5 liters)
Sugar (pounds)	3 (1.3 kg.)	4 (2 kg.)	5 (2.25 kg.)	6 (3 kg.)
Malt extract (pounds)	1 (450 g.)	2 (1 kg.)	3 (1.3 kg.)	4 (3 kg.)
Hops	1½ oz. (45 g.)	2 oz. (55 g.)	4-6 oz. (120-180 g.)	6-8 oz. (180-225 g.)
Days to clear	7	14	21	28
Keeps for	Weeks	Months	Months	Years
Use for each:	1 pkt. dried brewer's yeast			
	Water treatment as necessary			
	A good pinch of citric acid			
For stout:	Boil up ½ lb. (225 g.) patent black malt grains and 4 oz. (120 g.) flaked barley with the hops in Recipe 3 or 4			

The Procedure

Malt extract, as already pointed out, is the easiest ingredient to use because excellent results can be obtained from a cold brew, i.e., one where it is unnecessary to boil the whole of the wort. Most experienced brewers, however, do prefer to boil the whole wort to ensure its complete sterility, and to achieve clarity, as already explained. If you have a large enough boiler, there is no reason why all the ingredients should not be put in it and boiled together.

If your local water is soft, you will probably succeed best with milds, browns, and stouts, but if you wish to make a good pale ale or bitter, it will help if you add 1 teaspoon of plaster of Paris per 5 quarts (4.5 liters) of water. If your local water is hard, you will do best to make bitter or pale ale and will find it an advantage to boil all the water rather than to use the cold brew method. The addition of a little salt also helps.

Otherwise, bring to the boil as much water as your boiler will take, say 10 or 15 quarts, 9 or 13.5 liters (after room has been left for the hops and the vigor of the boiling). Add the malt extract, hops, water treatment, and coloring. You can darken the color of a beer by using caramel coloring (gravy browning liquid is useful, for it is only caramel, as you will see from the label) or by including some roasted barley or darker malts (this is how stouts get their color). The darker the malt, the more it contributes by way of color and the less to the strength.

Boil for at least forty-five minutes, adding a few extra hops in the last five minutes to restore aroma lost in boiling. Pour this wort into the fermenting vessel and make up with cold or warm water to the required final volume. Add a pinch of citric acid to ensure a quick start to fermentation. Leave enough room for the frothing that will take place. Allow to cool to 70°F (21°C) and then add yeast and nutrient.

With added malt and grits

Remember that if you are using grain malt or other grits to support your extract, and to improve the flavor (rather than just for coloring), you will need to follow a slightly different procedure, for in this case, you will need to observe the mashing principles for grain malt beers if you are to obtain the maximum value from your grain.

In this case, put the grain, the extract, and any water treatment being used into about half the water, say 7.5 quarts (6.5 liters), raise temperature to 150°F (65°C), and hold it closely to this temperature for about three-quarters of an hour.

Then add the hops, boil for half an hour, and strain onto any additional sugar, before making up to the required quantity with more water. Pale and crystal malts should be cracked, but heavily roasted malts should be used whole.

When the wort has cooled to 59°F (5°C), the yeast is pitched, and the fermentation, racking, fining, and bottling carried out in the usual way.

If using an open bin, cover with a thick cloth and rest the lid on top. The first head of froth that forms on the brew evidently carries up with it much of the aromatic oils of the hops, for if you taste it, you will see that it has a pronounced bitterness that lingers unpleasantly in the back of the throat, and your beer may later have this quality. So skim it off. It will only spoil the aroma and flavor of your beer if left to go into your brew. Wipe away the tideline also.

If, despite your precautions, you eventually produce a beer that is too bitter for your taste, the bitterness can be masked by the use of licorice. Dissolve a stick in a saucepan over the stove, with a little hot water, and add the resulting syrup to your brew a little at a time, until it seems to you that it has done the trick.

With a closed fermentation and a bottom yeast (one that works from the bottom), further skimming is unnecessary. After the initial frothing and the formation of the exciting corona, or ring, the head may turn a dirty brown. Do not worry about this. All is in order.

With strong beers, add half the sugar at the outset and the remainder after three days, stirring thoroughly. If all the sugar is used at the outset, they may stick at 1020 or so.

When the surface of the beer begins to clear, but bubbles collect in a ring in the center (or when the SG is below 1010, and as near as possible to 1000), you can bottle.

Dave Line devised many of the best recipes for this brewing method. Here are several of them, together with many of my own formulations as a guide to your experiments.

Malt Extract Beer Recipes

Lagers

Malt extract is not really well suited to the production of lager, because when using it, it is difficult to obtain the authentic light color usually expected in a lager. Here are some recipes, however, that give reasonably good results.

The critical factor in producing quality lager is a low fermenting temperature from start to finish (at no time above 65°F, 18°C, and preferably not above 60°F, 16°C). The fermentation should be under air lock, and a true lager bottom-fermenting yeast be chosen. The beer should be rested, on the lees, for at least a month at a temperature of about 45°F (7°C) and then be siphoned off and primed as usual.

Trojan Lager
(25 quarts/22.5 liters)

Ingredients		
2 lb.	Diastatic malt extract	1 kg.
2 lb.	Golden syrup	1 kg.
5	Saccharin tablets	
2 oz.	Hallertauer hops	55 g.
1 sachet	Lager yeast	
25 quarts	Water	22.5 liters

Method:
Follow instructions for Spartan Bitter (page 154).

Other useful lager formulations follow.

Light Lager

(20 quarts/18 liters)

Ingredients		
3½ lb.	Malt extract	1.6 kg.
3 lb	Sugar	1.3 kg.
2 oz.	Hallertauer hops	55 g.
	Lager yeast	
20 quarts	Water (soft)	18 liters
½ teaspoon	Citric acid	

Lager

(20 quarts/18 liters)

Ingredients		
5 lb.	Diastatic malt extract	2.25 kg.
4 lb.	Pale malt	2 kg.
4 lb.	Sugar	2 kg.
4 oz.	Saaz hops	100 g.
20 quarts	Water (soft)	18 liters
	Lager yeast	

Canadian Lager

(25 quarts/22.5 liters)

This recipe is for a lager specially suited to the Canadian palate.

Ingredients		
25 quarts	Water	22.5 liters
2½ lb.	Container of light barley malt extract	1 kg.
½ oz.	Kent finishing hops	15 g.
2 oz.	Branding or Cluster hops	55 g.
4 lb.	Corn sugar (dextrose)	2 kg.
1 teaspoon	Citric acid	
2-3 teaspoons	Salt	
½ teaspoon	Yeast energizer	
½ teaspoon	Special beer finings	
1 teaspoon	Heading liquid	
	Lager yeast	

Method:

Be sure to save 2 full cups of corn sugar for bottling, then make sure your yeast starter is ready to use. Boil as much of the water as possible. Naturally, this will depend on the size of the container you have, but not less than 5 quarts (4.5 liters). Along with the water, you should boil the malt extract, 2 oz. (55 g.) of hops (broken up and tied in cheesecloth), the salt, and citric acid. Simmer very gently for one to two hours with a lid on to reduce evaporation. As you remove this from the heat, add the ½ oz. (15 g.) of Kent hops, which can remain in the wort during the primary fermentation. Pour this hot wort over the corn sugar (minus the 2 cups, remember). Stir to dissolve the sugar and add the balance of the water to make up a total of 25 quarts (22.5 liters).

Cover the wort with a sheet of plastic tied down and allow the mixture to cool to around 60°F (15°C). This may take up to twelve hours, so don't hold your breath. The fermentation vessel should be in a place where the temperature will remain between 55°F and 65°F (12°C and 22°C). When the wort is cool, take a specific gravity reading to make sure it is between 1033 and 1038. (The starting gravity should be 1030 to 1040, and the beer should finish at 0, i.e., 1000.) If it is not correct, you can adjust it by adding more sugar or water, depending on whether it is high or low.

Now add the active lager yeast and cover once again with the plastic sheet. After about four or five days of active ferment, you can start checking the specific gravity to see how the ferment is progressing. It will probably take six to ten days to get down to between 1005 and 1010 depending on the temperature. When it gets to this point, skim off the floating hops, add the yeast energizer, and siphon the wort into the fermenter. Don't fill the fermenter too full, because you need room to add the finings at this point. Dissolve the ½ teaspoon of finings in 1 cup of very hot water (not boiling). Pour this on top of the beer in the fermenter and stir in thoroughly with the handle end of your wooden spoon. The fermenter should now be filled to within 2 or 3 in. (about 5-7 cm.) of the fermentation lock, which should be properly attached at this time.

Now that your beer is in the fermenter with the fermentation lock attached, place it in a cool place, 55°-65°F (12°-18°C), away from the light. It is safe even if you don't get to look at it for up to three weeks. Under normal circumstances, it will be clear and the gravity down to 1000 in about ten days. Don't worry about the extra time involved in making beer this way, inasmuch as your beer is aging in the fermenter and will be ready that much sooner after bottling. In any case, when these two things occur, i.e., the brew is reasonably clear and the gravity is down to 1000, the time has come for bottling.

Now take those 2 cups of sugar saved from your 4 lb. (2 kg.). Siphon off about 2 pints (1 liter) of beer into a clean saucepan, warm on the stove, and dissolve the 2 cups of sugar to make a beer sugar syrup. Be sure the saucepan is big enough, because the mixture will foam all over the stove if it's not. When this is ready, siphon off the rest of the beer into your clean primary fermenter, being careful not to disturb the yeast sediment.

Save your yeast. At this time, you can get your yeast back for your next brew by swirling the sediment in the bottom of the fermenter and, using a small funnel, pouring it into a clean beer bottle and capping immediately. Place this bottle in the crisper part of your refrigerator where it won't freeze. The next time you make beer, you will not have to grow your yeast, but merely take this bottle from the refrigerator, open it, and add it to the wort when the wort is properly cooled. This yeast starter will be good in the refrigerator for approximately three to five weeks in the case of lager yeast and two to three weeks for ale yeast.

Now that we have the clear beer in the primary fermenter and the gravity is 1000, stir in the syrup, making sure it is thoroughly distributed, but do not aerate the beer too much. At the same time, you can be stirring in the teaspoon of heading liquid. The gravity of this mixture should be approximately 1005. We will assume that you have already prepared your bottles, that they are thoroughly clean, and standing in a convenient place to be filled to within 1 in. (2.5 cm.) of the cap. It does not matter if they are wet inside, in fact, it may make it easier to fill them by reducing the foaming. Cap them immediately and place in a temperature of 60°-70°F (15°-20°C) for ten days and then chill and try the results of your labor.

For ale, use the same recipe with the addition of 1 oz. (30 g.) of gypsum, and ale instead of lager beer yeast.

Before it has completely worked, it is important to move the lager into a fermenter and attach a fermentation lock, or move it to glass or plastic demijohns. It should be lagered at a temperature of around 113°F (45°C), or lower, for at least one month, then carefully siphoned off the lees. Twelve oz. (340 g.) of corn sugar should be added to 25 quarts (22.5 liters), plus a teaspoon of heading liquid and a teaspoon of ascorbic acid. Then of course, it is essential, as all Canadian beer is normally bottled and crown capped, that the same procedure be followed here. It should stand in the bottle for at least three weeks to a month and is not likely to be at its peak much before three months from the outset of fermentation.

Patriarch Pilsner

(25 quarts/22.5 liters)

Ingredients		
2 tins (2½ lb. each)	Light malt extract	2.25 kg.
2 oz.	Brewers Gold or Cluster hops	55 g.
¼ oz.	Golding finishing	10 g.
4 lb.	Brewing (corn) sugar	2 kg.
25 quarts	Water	22.5 liters
2 teaspoons	Salt	
1 teaspoon	Citric acid	
1 teaspoon	Heading liquid	
½ teaspoon	Beer finings	
½ teaspoon	Grape tannin	
	Lager yeast (dry or liquid)	
	Starting gravity: 1043 to 1045	
	Terminal gravity: 1003	

Ingredients

Follow the instructions for Canadian Lager (page 135).

Dried malt extract

The dried powder malt extract on the market is more pleasant to handle than the sticky liquid variety, although it is a little more expensive.

In each of these German recipes, boil the dried malt and hops in the water for half an hour. Strain into fermentation jar or jars to take 10 quarts (9 liters), cool to 70°F (20°C), add yeast and nutrient, fit air lock, and leave to ferment in warm room for seven to eight days. Prime as directed under that heading, and bottle.

Light Lager: 2½ lb. (1 kg.) dried malt extract, 2 oz. (55 g.) hops, 10 quarts (9 liters) of water, beer yeast.

Lager (Pilsner-style): 4½ lb. (2 kg.) dried malt extract, 1 oz. (30 g.) hops, 10 quarts (9 liters) water, beer yeast.

Lager: (Munich style): 5 lb. (2.25 kg.) dried malt extract, ½ oz. (15 g.) caramel, 1 oz. (30 g.) hops, 20 quarts (18 liters) water, beer yeast.

Dark Beer or Porter: 6½ lb. (3.25 kg.) dried malt extract, 1 oz. (30 g.) caramel, 15 quarts (13.5 liters) water, beer yeast.

Ale: 6½ lb. (3.25 kg.) dried malt extract, 15 quarts (13.5 liters) water, 2 oz. (55 g.) hops, beer yeast.

Ales

Draught Pale Ale

(25 quarts/22.5 liters), Original Gravity 1037.

Ingredients		
3 lb.	Malt extract	1.3 kg.
1 lb.	Corn syrup	500 g.
2 lb.	Natural brown sugar	1 kg.
4 oz.	Goldings hops	100 g.
	Irish moss preparation	
	Beer yeast	
	Gelatin finings	
25 quarts	Water	22.5 liters

Method:

Follow instructions for Barley Mow Bitter (page 155).

'Lancaster' Light Ale

(20 quarts/18 liters)

Ingredients		
2 lb.	Edme diastatic malt extract	1 kg.
1 lb.	Soft dark brown sugar	450 g.
2 oz.	Goldings hops	55 g.
1 sachet	Edme beer yeast	
20 quarts	Water	18 liters

Method:

Follow instructions for Spartan Bitter (page 154).

Fallbright Light Ale

(20 quarts/18 liters)

Ingredients		
3.3 lb.	Mutona medium malt extract	1½ kg.
4 oz.	Crushed crystal malt	125 g.
1 lb.	Brewing (corn) sugar	500 g.
1 teaspoon	Yeast nutrient	
2 oz.	Golding hops	60 g.
	Heading liquid/powder	
	Beer yeast	
20 quarts	Water	18 liters

Method:

Dissolve the malt extract in 10 quarts (9 liters) of hot water. Add the crushed malt and hops and boil the mixture for forty-five minutes. Strain off the solids and add the brewing (corn) sugar to the hot liquid. Top up to the final quantity with cold water. When cool, pitch in the beer yeast and ferment four to five days. On the third day, add a requisite dose of heading agent. When the fermentation has almost stopped, add a tablespoon of sugar and leave for one more day before bottling in primed beer bottles.

Other formulations for 20 quarts (18 liters) of Light Ale follow.

Light Ale (1)

Ingredients		
6 lb.	Malt extract	3 kg.
2 lb.	Barley	1 kg.
1 tablespoon	Caramel	
3 oz.	Hallertauer hops	85 g.
20 quarts	Water (hard)	18 liters
½ teaspoon	Citric acid	
	Lager yeast	

Light Ale (2)

Ingredients		
5 lb.	Malt extract (DMS)	2.25 kg.
2 lb.	Pale malt	1 kg.
1 lb.	Flaked barley	450 g.
1 lb.	Brewing (corn) sugar	450 g.
4 oz.	Golding hops	100 g.
20 quarts	Water (hard)	18 liters
	Beer yeast	

Malthouse Mild

(25 quarts/22.5 liters), Original Gravity 1033

Ingredients		
2 lb.	Malt extract	1 kg.
2 lb.	Barley syrup	1 kg.
1½ lb.	Soft brown sugar	675 g.
2 tablespoons	Molasses	
3 oz.	Crushed black malt	85 g.
2 oz.	Fuggles hops	55 g.
10	Saccharin tablets	
	Irish moss preparation	
	Beer yeast	
	Gelatin finings	
25 quarts	Water	22.5 liters

Method:

Follow instructions for Barley Mow Bitter (page 155).

Blackmoor Mild Ale

(25 quarts/22.5 liters)

Ingredients		
4 lb.	Diastatic malt extract	2 kg.
2 lb.	White sugar	1 kg.
2 oz.	Crushed black malt	60 g.
3 teaspoons	Caramel	
2 oz. (approx.)	Hop extract	60 g. (approx.)
½ oz.	Dried brewer's yeast	15 g.
25 quarts	Water	22.5 liters

Method:

Boil the malt extract, black malt, and hop extract for thirty minutes in 10 quarts (9 liters) of water and strain off into the fermenting bin. Dissolve the sugar and caramel in boiling water and add this as well. Top up the bin to the final quantity with cold water. When cool to room temperature, pitch in the yeast and ferment four to five days before racking into a primed pressure barrel or fresh container.

Mild (draught)

(20 quarts/18 liters)

Ingredients		
4 lb.	Malt extract	2 kg.
2 lb.	Crystal malt	1 kg.
20 quarts	Water (soft)	18 liters
	Brewer's yeast	
1 lb.	Pale malt	450 g.
1½ lb.	Brewing (corn) sugar	675 g.
4 oz.	Fuggles hops	100 g.

Method:

Follow instructions for general boiling-up method in Blackmoor Mild Ale (above).

Nut Brown Ale

(25 quarts/22.5 liters)

Ingredients		
4 lb.	SFX malt extract (dark)	2 kg.
3 oz.	Crushed chocolate malt	100 g.
1 lb.	Light brown sugar	450 g.
2 oz.	Isomerized hop extract	60 g.
½ oz.	Fresh Northdown hops	15 g.
1 sachet	Dried beer yeast	
10	Saccharin tablets	
	Heading liquid	
25 quarts	Water	22.5 liters

Method:

Boil the malt extract, chocolate malt, and fresh hops for thirty minutes in 10-20 quarts (9-18 liters) of water. Strain off the solids into a fermenting bin. Top up to the final volume with cold water. When cool, add the hop extract, saccharin, and yeast. Ferment four to six days as required, rack off, and allow to settle under airlock protection for a few days before bottling in primed bottles to which one drop of heading liquid per pint (500 ml.) of capacity has been added. Sample after two weeks.

Brown Ale (1)

(20 quarts/18 liters)

Ingredients		
4 lb.	Malt extract	2 kg.
1½ lb.	Medium dark dried malt extract	675 g.
½ lb.	Sugar	225 g.
20 quarts	Water (soft)	18 liters
	Beer yeast	
½ lb.	Black malt	225 g.
½ oz.	Crystal malt	15 g.
1½ oz.	Fuggles hops	45 g.
1 lb.	Lactose dissolved in ½ pint (280 ml.) boiling water and added before bottling	450 g.

Method:

Follow instructions for Nut Brown Ale (page 145).

Brown Ale (2)

(20 quarts/18 liters)

Ingredients		
3 lb.	Malt extract	1.3 kg.
1 lb.	Brown sugar	450 g.
8 oz.	Black malt	225 g.
1½ oz.	Fuggles hops	45 g.
½ teaspoon	Salt	
20 quarts	Water (soft)	18 liters
	Brewer's yeast	

Method:

Follow instructions for Nut Brown Ale (page 145).

Sweet Brown Ale

(20 quarts/18 liters)

Ingredients		
3 lb.	Malt extract	1.3 kg.
1 lb.	Brown sugar	450 g.
2 oz.	Hops	55 g.
2 teaspoons	Yeast	
1 lb.	Lactose	450 g.
8 oz.	Black malt grains	225 g.
20 quarts	Water (soft)	18 liters

Note: The lactose is dissolved in half a pint (250 ml.) of boiling water, cooled, and added to the ale before bottling. This solution should be well stirred into the beer after racking. As it will not ferment, priming sugar is still needed.

Method:

Follow instructions for Nut Brown Ale (page 145).

Buckingham Brown Ale

(25 quarts/22.5 liters)

Ingredients		
2 lb.	Malt extract	1 kg.
1 lb.	Crushed crystal malt	450 g.
4 teaspoons	Caramel	
2 lb.	White sugar	1 kg.
8	Saccharin tablets	
2 oz.	Fuggles hops	55 g.
1 sachet	Beer yeast	
25 quarts	Water	22.5 liters

Method:

Follow instructions for Spartan Bitter (page 154).

Burton Brown Ale

(15 quarts/ 13.5 liters)

Ingredients		
2 lb.	SFX malt extract (dark)	1 kg.
3 oz.	Crushed black malt	100 g.
1 lb.	Glucose powder (or chips)	450 g.
1 oz.	Hops	30 g.
	Heading liquid/powder	
	Sweetex liquid	
	Beer yeast	
15 quarts	Water	13.5 liters

Method:

Follow instructions for Fallbright Light Ale (page 141), but add 24 drops of Sweetex with the heading liquid.

Dark Brown Ale

(20 quarts/18 liters)

Ingredients		
4 lb.	Malt extract	2 kg.
2 oz.	Hops	55 g.
4 sticks	Licorice, boiled	
1 lb.	Sugar	450 g.
20 quarts	Water (soft)	18 liters
	Stout yeast	

Strong Brown Ale

(20 quarts/18 liters)

Ingredients		
½ lb.	Milled black malt	225 g.
5 lb.	Malt extract	2.25 kg.
2 lb.	Brown sugar	1 kg.
4 oz.	Fuggles hops	120 g.
½ teaspoon	Citric acid	
20 quarts	Water (soft)	18 liters
	Brewer's yeast	

Bitters

5-Star Bitter

(25 quarts/22.5 liters)

Ingredients		
4 lb.	Tin malt extract	1.8 kg.
1 lb.	White sugar	450 g.
1 lb.	Golden syrup	450 g.
4 oz.	Hops (Goldings if named)	110 g.
1 sachet	Brewer's yeast	
10	Saccharin tablets	
	Gelatin finings	
25 quarts	Water	22.5 liters

Method:

1. Open the tins of extract and golden syrup and stand them in hot water for a few minutes to make them flow more easily.

2. Pour the extract into the saucepan and add as much water as possible. Leave at least 2 in. (about 5 cm.) of space to accommodate the sticky foam that forms during boiling.

3. Boil and then simmer the extract for fifteen minutes and then switch off. Add and stir in the hops. Repeat the stirring two or three more times over the next ten minutes.

4. Using a colander or large sieve, strain off the liquid wort from the hops into the fermentation bin. Rinse out the remaining absorbed extract from the hops with a couple of pots of hot water.

5. Dissolve the golden syrup and sugar in hot water and add this to the wort as well. Top up the bin to the 25-quart (22.5 liter) mark with cold water.

6. Add the yeast, saccharin tablets, and finings, replace the lid, and store the bin in a warm place (around 70°F, 20°C) for the fermentation to start.

7. The yeast will start to form a thick frothy foam over the surface as fermentation progresses. Skim off any dirty scum that forms and stir daily until the activity diminishes and the beer starts to clear at the surface. Usually fermentation is complete after five or six days.

8. Prime and bottle or cask.

Brewster Bitter

(25 quarts/22.5 liters), Original Gravity 1039

Ingredients		
4 lb.	Medium malt extract	2 kg.
4 oz.	Crushed crystal malt	125 g.
2 oz.	Crushed wheat malt	60 g.
2 lb.	White sugar	1 kg.
2 oz.	Goldings hops	60 g.
1 oz.	Hallertauer hops	30 g.
1 sachet	Beer yeast	
	Pale ale/bitter water treatment salts	
25 quarts	Water	22.5 liters

Method:

Boil the malt extract with the hops for forty-five minutes. Pitch in the crushed grain for the last five minutes.

Meanwhile:

Dissolve the sugar in boiling water and pour into a sterilized fermenting bin. Also make up a yeast starter with a little cooled wort solution.

Then:

Switch off the boiler and allow the cooked wort to stand for five minutes. Strain off as much of the clear liquid as possible into the fermenting bin. Add a pot of hot water to the redundant solids in the boiling pan and allow to stand again. Straining off this time should retrieve most of the absorbed extract.

Top the fermenting bin up to the final quantity with cold water and allow to cool to room temperature before pitching in the yeast starter. Ferment four to eight days until the SG falls to around 1006. Remove surface scum on the brew and drop in two crushed Campden (food grade sodium metabisulphite) tablets. Snap on the lid and leave two days undisturbed.

Bottle or cask as appropriate, priming at the rate of ½ teaspoon per pint (5 ml. per liter) or ½ oz. per 5 quarts (3 g. per liter).

Sample casked beer after ten days and bottled brews after three weeks.

Marksman Bitter
(25 quarts/22.5 liters)

Ingredients		
4 lb.	Malt extract	1 kg.
3 lb.	Crushed pale malt	1.3 kg.
5 oz.	Flaked corn	150 g.
2 teaspoons	Brewers caramel	
1 lb.	Brewing (corn) sugar	450 g.
2 oz.	Goldings hops	60 g.
1 oz. approx.	Styrian Goldings isomerized hop extract	30 g. approx.
	Few drops of hop oil essence	
½ oz.	Dried brewer's yeast	15 g.
½ oz.	Davis gelatin	15 g.
	Pale ale water treatment	
25 quarts	Water	22.5 liters

Method:

1. Add the water treatment to 5 quarts (4.5 liters) of water and raise its temperature to around 140°F (60°C). Add the crushed malt grains and flakes. Stir continuously and raise the temperature to 155°F (67°C) before switching off the heat. Maintain the temperature as close to 150°F (65°C) for two hours. Strain off the sweet wort and rinse the grains to collect 15 quarts (13.5 liters) of wort.

2. Boil the wort with the Goldings hops for one hour and then strain off into the fermenting vessel.

3. Boil the malt extract, brewing (corn) sugar, and caramel in sufficient water for a few minutes, and add this to the fermenting bin as well. Top up the bin to the final quantity with cold water. When cool to room temperature, pitch in the yeast and hop extract.

4. Ferment four to five days or as necessary for the SG to fall to 1008 and rack the brew into a fresh container.

5. Rest the beer for a week and fine with gelatin.

6. Rack into pressure barrel and prime with 1½ oz. (45 g.) of sugar.

Spartan Bitter

(25 quarts/22.5 liters)

Ingredients		
3 lb.	Boots malt extract	1.3 kg.
1 lb.	Natural brown sugar	450 g.
5	Saccharin tablets	
2 oz.	Hops (Goldings or Fuggles)	55 g.
1 sachet	Beer yeast	
25 quarts	Water	22.5 liters

Method:

1. Boil the malt extract in 5 quarts (4.5 liters) or so of water for forty-five minutes. Include any crushed grain, caramel, or whole hops in the boil as well.

2. Strain off into a fermenting bin and add the saccharin tablets and hop extract as required. Also stir in the golden syrup or sugar (previously dissolved in a little boiling water) before topping up the bin to the final quantity with cold water.

3. Add the yeast when cool and ferment for three to four days.

4. Rack off into 5-quart (4.5 liter) jars or fresh containers fitted with an airlock, and leave the beer to clear. Gelatin finings may be used to hasten the clarification.

5. When clear, siphon off into primed beer bottles or a pressure barrel and leave one week before sampling.

Barley Mow Bitter

(25 quarts/22.5 liters), Original Gravity 1035

Ingredients			
2 lb.	Malt extract		1 kg.
2 lb.	Barley syrup		1 kg.
2 lb.	Golden syrup		1 kg.
4 oz.	Goldings hops		100 g.
	Irish moss preparation		
	Beer yeast		
	Gelatin finings		
25 quarts	Water		22.5 liters

Method:

1. Boil the malt extract, barley or corn syrup, and Irish moss in 10 quarts of water for twenty minutes. Then switch off.

2. Stir in the hops and stir occasionally over the next ten minutes.

3. Strain off the wort from the hops into a fermentation vessel.

4. Dissolve the golden syrup, sugar, or molasses as appropriate in hot water and add this to the bin as well. Top up the bin to the 25-quart (4.5 liter) mark with cold water.

5. When cooled to 70°F (21°C), add the yeast and saccharin tablets if used and ferment in a warm place for four to five days. Skim off any dirty yeast.

6. Rack off into a fresh container or 5-quart jars and add gelatin finings. Leave two days to clear.

7. Rack off again into 25-quart (4.5 liter) pressure barrel. Add 2 tablespoons of sugar or preferably golden syrup for priming. Fit an injector unit or plain cap fitted with a safety valve as preferred.

8. Sample for clarity and condition after one week.

More malt extract formulations worth trying follow.

Bitter (1)

(20 quarts/18 liters)

Ingredients		
3 lb.	Malt extract	1.3 kg.
1 lb.	White sugar	450 g.
3 oz.	Hops	85 g.
1 tablespoon	Caramel coloring	
20 quarts	Water (hard)	18 liters
½ teaspoon	Citric acid	
2 teaspoons	Dried beer yeast	

Bitter (2)

(20 quarts/18 liters)

Ingredients		
4 lb.	Malt extract	2 kg.
8 tablespoons	Medium dark dried malt extract	
4 oz.	Hops	100 g.
1½ lb.	Granulated sugar	675 g.
20 quarts	Water (hard)	18 liters
	Brewer's yeast	

Bitter (3)

(25 quarts/22.5 liters)

Ingredients		
6 lb.	Malt extract	3 kg.
3 lb.	Pale malt	1.3 kg.
3 lb.	Sugar	1.3 kg.
6 oz.	Golding hops	180 g.
20 quarts	Water (hard)	18 liters
	Brewer's yeast	

Berry Brew (Best Bitter)

(25 quarts/22.5 liters)

Ingredients		
4 lb.	Malt extract	2 kg.
1½ lb.	Sugar	680 g.
1 teaspoon	Citric acid	
2 teaspoons	Salt	
25 quarts	Water	22.5 liters
4 oz.	Golding hops	100 g.
1 tablespoon	Caramel	
	Gravy browning liquid boiled with hops	
	Brewer's yeast	

Stouts

Star Stout (sweet)
(25 quarts/22.5 liters)

Ingredients		
5 lb.	Diastatic malt extract	2.25 kg.
1 lb.	Crushed chocolate malt	450 g.
2 lb.	Natural brown sugar	1 kg.
15	Saccharin tablets	
2 oz.	Fuggles hops	60 g.
1 oz. (approx.)	Isomerized hop extract	30 g. (approx.)
½ oz.	Dried beer yeast	15 g.
25 quarts	Water	22.5 liters

Method:

Boil the malt extract, crushed grain, and whole hops in 10 quarts (9 liters) of water for forty-five minutes. Strain off into a fermenting bin and stir in the quota of sugar and hop extract. Top up to the final quantity with cold water before sprinkling in the beer yeast. Ferment until the SG falls to 1004 and bottle in primed beer bottles. Mature for ten days before sampling.

Extra Stout (dry)

(25 quarts/22.5 liters)

Ingredients		
5 lb.	Diastatic malt extract	2.25 kg.
1 lb.	Crushed roast barley	500 g.
2 lb.	White sugar	1 kg.
2 oz.	Hops	60 g.
2 oz. (approx.)	Bullion isomerized hop extract	60 g. (approx.)
½ oz.	Dried beer yeast	15 g.
25 quarts	Water	22.5 liters

Method:

Follow instructions for Star Stout (page 158).

Black Barrel Stout

(20 quarts/18 liters)

Ingredients		
4 lb.	Malt extract	2 kg.
1 lb.	Crushed crystal malt	450 g.
½ lb.	Crushed black malt	225 g.
2 lb.	Golden syrup	1 kg.
20	Saccharin tablets	
2 oz.	Hops	50 g.
	Brewer's yeast	
20 quarts	Water	18 liters

Method:

Boil the malt extract, hops, and grain (if required) in 10 quarts (9 liters) of water for forty-five minutes. Strain off into fermenting bin and rinse with another 2 quarts (2 liters) of hot water. Dissolve the golden syrup in a few pints (500 ml.

or more) of hot water and add this to the bin as well. Top up to the required amount with cold water. When the wort is cool, add the yeast and saccharin tablets.

Ferment for four to five days and then rack off and fine with gelatin before casking or bottling the beer as required.

Porter

(20 quarts/18 liters)

Ingredients		
2 lb.	Malt extract	1 kg.
1 lb.	Black malt	450 g.
1 lb.	Flaked barley	450 g.
2 lb.	White sugar	1 kg.
20 quarts	Water (soft)	18 liters
3 oz.	Fuggles hops	85 g.
	Brewer's yeast	

Stout

(20 quarts/18 liters)

Ingredients		
3 lb.	Malt extract	1.3 kg.
½ lb.	Pale malt	225 g.
1 lb.	Patent black malt boiled with 3 oz. (90 g.) hops for thirty minutes	450 g.
2 lb.	Dark brown sugar	1 kg.
1 teaspoon	Salt	
20 quarts	Water (soft)	18 liters
	Stout yeast	

Oatmeal Stout

(20 quarts/18 liters)

Ingredients		
6 lb.	Malt extract	3 kg.
1 lb.	Black malt	450 g.
2 lb.	Oatmeal	1 kg.
4 lb.	Sugar	2 kg.
8 oz.	Lactose	225 g.
6 oz.	Fuggles hops	150 g.
20 quarts	Water (soft)	18 liters
	Cultured stout yeast	

Dissolve lactose in half pint (250 ml.) of boiling water, cool, and stir well into the bulk before bottling.

Double Stout

(22.5 quarts/20 liters)

Ingredients		
5½ lb.	Diastatic malt extract	2.5 kg.
1 lb.	Black malt, cracked	450 g.
12 oz.	Flaked barley	300 g.
2 teaspoons	Salt	
22.5 quarts	Water (soft)	20 liters
4 oz.	Fuggles hops	100 g.
	Cultured stout yeast	

CHAPTER 13

NOVELTY BEERS

True beer, of course, is that made from malt and hops, but there are many other "beers," many of them delightful drinks in their own right and some of them of undoubted therapeutic value. It is fun to experiment and produce unusual drinks not available at the local beer distributer.

Novelty Beer Recipes

Apple Ale

Here is a very old recipe for a cider-like ale.
(5 quarts/4.5 liters)

Ingredients		
3 lb.	Apples (windfalls will do)	1.3 kg.
1 oz.	Root ginger	30 g.
½ teaspoon	Cloves	
12 teaspoons	Cinnamon	
1½ lb.	White sugar	675 g.
5 quarts	Water	4.5 liters
	Yeast and nutrient	

Method:

Wash the apples, cutting out any damaged portions, and grate or mince. Add the water, cold, and the yeast and nutrient. Cover with a thick cloth and leave in a warm room for a week, stirring thoroughly daily. Strain onto the sugar, bruised ginger, cloves, and cinnamon, and press out as much extra juice from the pulp as possible by squeezing it in a cloth. Stir vigorously, cover, and leave for about five days. Strain into screw-stoppered flagons or plastic resealed pint bottles. Store in a cool place and the ale will be ready to drink in about two weeks.

Brahn Ale

(15 quarts/13.5 liters)

Ingredients		
1 lb.	Bran	450 g.
2 oz.	Hops	55 g.
2 lb.	Natural brown sugar	1 kg.
	Gravy browning liquid	
	Yeast and nutrient	
15 quarts	Water	13.5 liters

Method:

Put 10 quarts (9 liters) of water in a 15-quart (13.5 liter) boiler. Bring to boil. Add sugar, hops, bran, and 2 teaspoons of gravy browning liquid. Boil gently for an hour and a half. Strain through muslin into fermenter and add 1.5 quarts (1 liter) of cold water. Leave to cool until blood heat (98.6°F, 37°C), then pour into three 5-quart (4.5 liters) jars, filling to shoulder only. Add brewer's yeast, if obtainable, or dried yeast. Fit traps and leave for seven days (in room temperature). Then siphon into strong beer bottles and cork or seal very tightly. The beer may be drunk after another week, but will not be really clear. To clarify, it should be kept at least three weeks after bottling in a cool place. This is an excellent and inexpensive ale and may be made week by week to accumulate a quantity, each fresh brew being put on to part of the less of the former one, and the surplus yeast thrown away or used for other purposes. If this system is to be followed, it pays to obtain a small quantity of true brewer's yeast initially, and it can then be kept going for several months.

Cider

Any apples will do, windfall or otherwise, but cider apples or cooking apples are best. Wash them, and then chop them into small pieces with a chopping knife, or crush them with an apple-crusher, or with a piece of heavy timber in a half-tub. Press out the juice with a press or by means of a juice extractor, and fill your fermenting vessel. Keep a little spare juice in a separate covered jug for "topping up." After a few days, if kept in a warm place, the juice will start fermenting. The container should be stood on a tray because, for a while, froth will pour out of the neck of the jar. Wipe this off and keep the jar topped up with the surplus juice. When the ferment quiets, wipe the jar and tray clean and fit a fermentation trap. When fermentation has ceased, bottle in screw-stopper flagons or strong bottles with plastic reseals.

Dandelion Beer

(5 quarts/4.5 liters)

Ingredients		
½ lb.	Young dandelion plants	225 g.
1 lb.	Natural brown sugar	450 g.
1	Lemon	
	Yeast	
5 quarts	Water	4.5 liters
½ oz.	Root ginger	15 g.
1 oz.	Cream of tartar	30 g.

Method:

This is a pleasant drink and is said to be good for stomach disorders. The young plants should be lifted in the spring and well washed. Leave the thick taproots, but remove the fibrous ones. Put the plants, the well-bruised ginger, and the rind of the lemon (excluding any white pith) in the water and boil for twenty minutes. Strain onto the sugar, the juice of the lemon, and cream of tartar. Stir until all is dissolved. Cool to 70°F (20°C), add yeast, and ferment (covered) in a warm place for three days. Bottle in screw-stopper bottles or plastic-resealed pint bottles.

Elderflower Beer

(5 quarts/4.5 liters)

Ingredients		
1 pint	Elderflowers (not pressed down)	570 ml.
5 quarts	Water	4.5 liters
1	Lemon	
1 lb.	Sugar	450 g.
	Yeast and nutrient	

Method:

Squeeze out the lemon juice and put into a bowl with the elder florets and sugar. Then pour the boiling water over them. Infuse for twenty-four hours, closely covered, then add yeast. Ferment for a week in a warm room, then strain into screw-stopper flagons or plastic-resealed pint bottles. Store in a cool place for a week, after which the beer will be ready for drinking.

Ginger Beer

(5 quarts/4.5 liters)

Ingredients		
1 oz.	Root ginger	30 g.
½ oz.	Cream of tartar	15 g.
1 lb.	White sugar	450 g.
1	Lemon	
5 quarts	Water	4.5 liters
	Yeast and nutrient	

Method:

The ginger should be crushed and then placed in a bowl with the sugar, cream of tartar, and lemon peel (no white pith). Bring the water to the boil and pour it over the ingredients. Stir well to dissolve the sugar, then allow to cool to 70°F (20°C) before adding the lemon juice, yeast, and nutrient.

Cover closely and leave in a warm room for forty-eight hours, then stir, strain into screw-stopper flagons or plastic-resealed pint bottles, and store in a cool place. The beer is ready to drink in three to four days.

How to Start a Ginger Beer Plant

(This is an old but amusing recipe.)

Grow a ginger beer plant with 2 oz. (55 g.) baker's yeast. Use fresh baker's yeast if you can. Put the yeast into a jar and add ½ pint (280 ml.) water, 2 teaspoons of sugar, and 2 teaspoons of ground ginger.

Feed it each day for the next seven to ten days by adding 1 teaspoon of sugar and 1 teaspoon of ground ginger. You will see your "plant" growing day by day.

Strain it. Now strain the mixture through a piece of muslin or a very fine household sieve (keep the sediment) and add to the liquid the juice of 2 lemons, 1 lb. (450 g.) granulated sugar, and 1 pint (570 ml.) boiling water. Stir until the sugar has dissolved, then make up to 5 quarts (4.5 liters) with cold water.

Bottle it. Put the ginger pop into strong bottles, filling to about 3 in. (75 mm.) from the top. Leave for two hours, taking care not to put them on a stone floor, unless standing on a piece of wood. Then cork lightly or seal with plastic reseals. Keep for seven to ten days before drinking.

And start again. The sediment you had left when you strained the mixture is divided into two and put into separate glass jars, and you're back in the brewing business again. But now you have two plants instead of one. If one plant is enough for you, give the other to a friend and give him the recipe. To your sediment add ½ pint (250 ml.) of cold water and follow the instructions onward from "Feed it each day."

Honey Botchard

This is a beer-strength mead.

(5 quarts/4.5 liters)

Ingredients		
1 oz.	Hops	30 g.
1¼ lb.	Honey	560 g.
5 quarts	Water	4.5 liters
	Yeast and nutrient	

Method:

Bring the water to the boil, add the hops and honey, and simmer for thirty minutes. Strain the liquid, allow to cool to 70°F (20°C), and add yeast and nutrient. Ferment in a warm room for ten days, then siphon into screw-stopper flagons or plastic-resealed pint bottles. Store in a cool place for at least a month.

Hop Beer (1)

(15 quarts/13.5 liters)

Ingredients		
5 oz.	Hops	140 g.
15 quarts	Water	13.5 liters
3 lb.	Brown sugar	1.3 kg.
2 teaspoons	Granulated yeast and nutrient	

Method:

Boil the hops and water together slowly for about forty to fifty minutes. Strain over the sugar and allow to cool. When tepid, add the yeast. Strain into 5-quart (4.5 liter) jars to ferment for four days at 65°F (17°C). Leave it to ferment up to a week if the temperature is lower. Bottle using crown cork or plastic reseal bottles. Can be drunk within two weeks, but may take a month really to clear.

Hop Beer (2)

(5 quarts/4.5 liters)

Ingredients		
½ oz.	Hops	15 g.
1 lb.	White sugar	450 g.
½ teaspoon	Caramel	
5 quarts	Water	4.5 liters
½ oz.	Root ginger, crushed	15 g.
	Yeast and nutrient	

Method:

Boil all the ingredients except yeast in the water for an hour, and then make up to 5 quarts (4.5 liters) if necessary. Strain, cool to 70°F (20°C), and add yeast and nutrient. Leave forty-eight hours in a warm place, closely covered, then siphon off (without disturbing yeast deposit) into screw-stopper flagons or plastic-resealed pint bottles. Stand in a cool place. Ready to drink in a week.

Nettle Beer

(10 quarts/9 liters)

Ingredients		
10 quarts	Young nettles	9 liters
¼ oz.	Root ginger	10 g.
4 lb.	Malt	2 kg.
1 teaspoon	Granulated yeast	
2 oz.	Hops	55 g.
4 oz.	Sarsaparilla	100 g.
10 quarts	Water	9 liters
1½ lb.	Sugar	675 g.
2	Lemons	

Method:

Choose young nettle tops. Wash and put into a saucepan with water, ginger, malt, hops, and sarsaparilla. Bring to the boil and boil for a quarter of an hour. Put sugar into a bucket and strain the liquor onto it. Add the juice of the two lemons. Stir until the sugar has dissolved, and allow to cool to 70°F (20°C), keeping bucket covered. Then stir in the yeast. Keep the bucket (covered) in a warm room for three days, then strain the beer into bottles (plastic seal or crown cork). Keep the beer in a cool place for a week before drinking—and keep an eye on the stoppers. This makes an excellent summer drink and should be made in May.

Parsnip Stout

(5 quarts/4.5 liters)

Ingredients		
3⅓ lb.	Parsnips	1.6 kg.
5 quarts	Water	4.5 liters
1 oz.	Hops	30 g.
½ lb.	Malt extract	225 g.
	Yeast	
2 tablespoons	Gravy browning liquid or 4 oz. (115 g.) black malt	
1¼ lb.	Natural brown sugar	560 g.

Method:

Scrub the parsnips and slice them in ½-in. (10 mm.) slices. Bring the water to the boil, add the parsnips, hops, and caramel coloring (or black malt), and boil for twenty minutes. Then strain onto the malt extract and sugar. Stir well to dissolve. Cool to 70°F (20°C), then add yeast and nutrient. Cover well and leave in a warm place for seven days. Then siphon into screw-stopper flagons or plastic-resealed pint bottles and store in a cool larder for two weeks before drinking.

Spruce Beer

(5 quarts/4.5 liters)

Spruce essence is difficult to obtain nowadays, but rewarding if you can find it.

To make the beer the recipe is as follows:

Melt 2 lb. (1 kg.) sugar, treacle, malt extract, molasses, or honey, into 5 quarts (4.5 liters) of cold water and 4 tablespoons of the essence of spruce. (Spruce essence can be purchased from winemaking supply firms and from some branches of principal chain chemists.) When the must is tepid, add ale yeast. Ferment for three days, then bottle. It will be ready for use within one week.

Treacle Ale

(5 quarts/4.5 liters)

Ingredients		
½ lb.	Golden syrup	225 g.
½ lb.	Black treacle	225 g.
½ lb.	Natural brown sugar	225 g.
1 oz.	Hops	30 g.
5 quarts	Water	4.5 liters
	Yeast and nutrient	

Method:

Bring the water to the boil, add the hops, syrup, treacle, and sugar, and simmer for forty-five minutes. Strain, cool to 70°F (20°C), add yeast and nutrient, and ferment for at least a week before bottling in screw-stopper flagons or plastic-resealed pint bottles.

Rooster Ale

In a one-hundred-year-old book on brewing, we came across the following recipe for a fearsome brew, Rooster Ale, also known as Cock Ale in the UK.

Take 50 quarts (45 liters) of ale and a large rooster, the older the better. Parboil the rooster, flay it, and stamp it in a stone mortar until the bones are broken (you must draw and gut it when you flay it). Then put the rooster into a 2-quart (2 liter) sack. Add 5 lb. (2.25 kg.) raisins of the sun, stoned, some blades of mace, and a few cloves. Put all these into a canvas bag, and a little before you find the ale has been working, put the bag and ale together into a vessel. In a week or nine days, bottle it up. Fill the bottle just above the neck and give it the same time to ripen as other ale.

Rather amusedly, and entirely by way of experiment, it was decided to try this, on a 5-quart (4.5 liter) quantity. Astonishingly, it made an excellent ale, nourishing and strong-flavored, of the "barley wine" type.

Many years later we heard of the old practice of putting a joint of meat into a barrel of cider—where it disappeared—in order to produce a really strong brew. It has been discovered that there was, in fact, a good scientific basis for this, in that it greatly increased the protein content of the brew. So it's worth trying.

All you need are some pieces of cooked chicken and a few chicken bones, all well crushed or minced (about a tenth of the eatable portion of the bird), ½ pound (225 g.) of raisins, a very little mace, and 1 or, if you like, 2 cloves. Soak these for twenty-four hours in half a bottle of your strongest white country wine.

Then make 5 quarts (4.5 liters) of beer as described in our malt extract section using 1 lb. (450 g.) malt extract, 1 oz. (30 g.) hops, ½ lb. (225 g.) natural brown sugar, 5 quarts (4.5 liters) water, yeast, and nutrient. Add the whole of your rooster mixture to the fermenting wort at the end of the second day. Fermentation will last six or seven days longer than usual and the ale should be matured at least a month in bottle.

CHAPTER 14

SERVING YOUR BEERS

The rule is, drink when clear, serve cool. There is bound to be some sediment, which will cloud the drink if carelessly poured. For example, if your beer is in a pint (500 ml.) bottle, have a jug of larger capacity handy, or more than one pint (500 ml.) tankard, to allow for any extra foaming so that you can pour continuously without having to return the bottle to the vertical. Open the bottle with caution in case you have over-primed the bottle.

Hold the jug or other receptacle at a slant in one hand, and gently tilt the bottle in the other so that the beer slides out slowly against the side of it.

Avoid the uneven flow that comes of pouring too fast. This will stir up the sediment. Watch the color of the beer as you pour and stop the flow smartly as soon as you see it becoming cloudy. You will be left with up to an inch of yeasty beer in the bottom of the bottle. Drink it down yourself and know what good health is, or pour it into a spare bottle, with other dregs, to settle. If you bungle the pouring and the drink is cloudy, don't apologize. You are only giving others a share in the most nourishing part of the brew instead of keeping it for yourself.

Lively Beer

Sometimes in spring or summer, usually at the onset of a warm spell, you will get an extra vigorous fermentation in the flagon, so that the beer is over-lively. When you unscrew a stopper or remove a crown cap there may even be a loud noise instead of a gentle hiss, and the beer will foam out vigorously. At times, it will send up a spout of foaming beer like a fountain. And (what is perhaps even worse, in a beer drinker's opinion) all the yeast sediment will rise and make the beer horribly cloudy and temporarily undrinkable.

There is only one solution. Clean the bottles and stand them in the sink. Then release the stoppers and let the bottles foam naturally. Let the process continue until no more froth issues from the bottles (although there may still be a head inside them). Then screw down once more or fit fresh crown caps. Wipe the bottles clean and store for forty-eight hours, by which time the beer will be clear again, and drinkable, its liveliness normal.

Not much beer will be lost, except in severe cases, for usually only foam comes out, but even this can be saved and poured back into the bottles if you stand the flagons in a clean bowl (not one that has held detergent) or brewing bucket and collect the overflow.

Another way is to insert a cork and length of tubing into each bottle and drain off the froth into fresh containers as is done with casks that are too lively.

Exhibiting and Judging

Brewing has now attained the same stature as winemaking as regards competitions, for the National Guild of Wine and Beer Judges (UK) now includes a most useful chapter on beer judging in its handbook for judges, show organizers, and competitors (*Judging Wine and Beer*).

The guild sets out the main types of beer, and their characteristics, and explains what the judge will be looking for—clean sound bottles, clean closures (now usually gold-colored crown caps), an air space of ½ in. to 1 in. (1.5-2.5 cm.), a firm yeast deposit, a good head and head retention coupled with a small and lively "bead" (the bubbles), a satisfactory aroma, and the correct body and flavor for that particular type of beer. Normally, points will be awarded based on categories such as presentation, clarity and sediment, color, head and condition, bouquet, and flavor and balance.

You may care not only to become an exhibitor, but eventually to become a judge as well, for judges are in great demand in the UK. Again, the handbook will be your guide to success, and you will eventually be able to take the Guild's qualifying examination.

In the United States, with 19,000 members and growing, the American Homebrewers Association conducts a national competition for homebrewers of beer, and statewide competitions are held in many of the 50 states.

INDEX

More Books from Fox Chapel Publishing

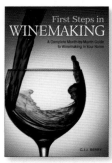

First Steps in Winemaking
A Complete Month-by-Month Guide to Winemaking in Your Home
By C. J. J. Berry

Delve into the world of at-home winemaking with methods and techniques that will turn your kitchen into a vineyard.

ISBN: 978-1-56523-602-8
$14.95 • 232 Pages

130 New Winemaking Recipes
Make Delicious Wine at Home Using Fruits, Grains, and Herbs
By C. J. J. Berry

Follow these 130 classic recipes for making wine in your own kitchen using traditional country ingredients.

ISBN: 978-1-56523-600-4
$12.95 • 136 Pages

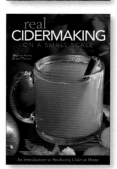

Real Cidermaking on a Small Scale
An Introduction to Producing Cider at Home
By Michael Pooley and John Lomax

Discover everything you need to know about making hard cider from any kind of apple—whether from your backyard or the local supermarket.

ISBN: 978-1-56523-604-2
$12.95 • 136 Pages

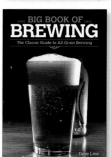

Big Book of Brewing
The Classic Guide to All-Grain Brewing
By Dave Line

Brewing your own beer is easier than you think with the easy-to-follow instructions in this book that will teach you the simple "mashing" technique that produces the finest flavored beers, ales, stouts, and lagers.

ISBN: 978-1-56523-603-5
$17.95 • 256 Pages